# 1963

# THE NEWS
# THE EVENTS
# AND
# THE LIVES
# OF 1963

Elizabeth Absalom & Malcolm Watson

D'AZUR PUBLISHING

Published by D'Azur Publishing 2022
D'Azur Publishing is a Division of D'Azur Limited

First published in Great Britain in 2022 by D'Azur Publishing
A Division of D'Azur Limited
Contact: info@d-azur.com  Visit www.d-azur.com
ISBN 9798848765977

## ACKNOWLEDGEMENTS
The publisher wishes to acknowledge the following people and sources:

British Newspaper Archive; The Times Archive ; p22 Yahoo Entertainment; p25 The Great Ocean Liners;p29 SolentForts.com;p31 Antikbar; p31 army apprentice college chepstow;p37 The Art Of Manliness; p39 Triang;p43 5sqft; p45 Classic And Sports Cars; p45 Classic World;p49 Victorian Era;p49 Taylor Lynn Corporation; p49 etiquipedia;p55 de364.org; p55 Business Insider; p55 Voval Media;p61 The Theatre Trust; p61 IMGUR; p63 NASA; p65 Antipodean.com; p67 RLBI David Jenkins; p67 Estate of Wallace A S Fuggle; p67 RNLI/Robbie McKennan;p71 NewsFlicks;p73 Thames Match;p75 Foreign and Commonwealth Office; p75 cbg Numistics; p81 Marion Bradshaw; p81 Down East; p83 Design Council / University of Brighton Design Archives;p85 Kelly Sikkema on Unsplash p85 Button and Snap; p85 Anything Left Handed;p87 Jose Antonio Gallego Vázquez on Unsplashp89 Chris Heaton; p89 Port of London Authority; p91 Ships Nostalgia; p91 Cruise Critic; p97 Dustin Humes on Unsplash; p97 Andre Klimke on Unsplash; p101 The Spruce Eats; p101 The Wine Anorak; p103 Ruskins Trees and Landscapes; p103 Green Ecp Friend; p105 Australian Customs and Border Protection Service; p105 Stefan Powel; p115 Met Office; p119 Kevin Schmid on Unsplash; p121 London Metropolitan Archives; p127 The Global Granary;

Whilst we have made every effort to contact copyright holders, should we have made any omission, please contact us so that we can make the appropriate acknowledgement.

# CONTENTS

# HIGHLIGHTS

Monarch - Queen Elizabeth II

Prime Minister Harold Macmillan until October 19th then Alec Douglas-Home. Both Conservative.

In 1963 Harold Macmillan was presiding over a period where individual events made it a watershed in Britain's post war history. In June, in the aftermath of the biggest scandal in politics, the 'Profumo Affair', he was so bewildered by the madness of this new age that he could only brokenly stammer to the Commons, 'I do not live among young people fairly widely.'

Labour MPs were clamouring for him to resign, and his own party hastened his political doom. It was the end of the 'old order'; the winter of the Big Freeze; Saturday night satire with TW3; President de Gaulle slamming the door on joining the Common Market; Dr Beeching closing the railways; the Great Train Robbery; Polaris; Dr Who appearing and the assassination of John F Kennedy.

But perhaps, it was mostly the Year of the Beatles. The mop-topped four released their first album, 'Please Please Me' and Beatlemania taking hold across Britain.

## FAMOUS PEOPLE WHO WERE BORN IN 1963

26th Jan: José Mourinho, football manager
17th Feb: Alison Hargreaves, British climber
27th Mar: Quentin Tarantino, film maker
8th April: Julian Lennon, Singer
11th May: Natasha Richardson, British actress
25th June: George Michael, British singer
3rd July: Tracey Emin, British artist
3rd Nov: Ian Wright, British footballer
5th Dec: Eddie 'The Eagle' Edwards, skier

## FAMOUS PEOPLE WHO DIED IN 1963

18th Jan: Hugh Gaitskell, British politician
29th Jan: Robert Frost, American poet
11th Feb: Sylvia Plath, American poet
5th Mar: Patsy Cline, American singer
22nd Aug: William Morris, founder, Morris cars
10th Oct: Edith Piaf, French singer
22nd Nov: John F Kennedy, President, USA
22nd Nov: Aldous Huxley, Author
22nd Nov: CS Lewis, Irish born British writer

# OF THE YEAR

**JANUARY**      French President Charles de Gaulle vetoes the United Kingdom's entry into the European Common Market.

**FEBRUARY**      Travel, financial and commercial transactions by US citizens to Cuba are made illegal.
Harold Wilson becomes the leader of the opposition Labour Party in the UK.

**MARCH**      Mount Agung erupts on Bali killing approximately 1,500 people.
Dr Richard Beeching, Chairman of British Railways releases his report calling for huge cuts to the UK's rail network.

**APRIL**      Yugoslavia is proclaimed to be a socialist republic and Tito is named President for Life.
The Polaris Sales Agreement is made with the US leading to the construction of nuclear submarine facilities at Faslane Naval Base.

**MAY**      The Coca-Cola company introduces its first diet drink, Tab cola.
The Profumo Affair in the UK brings about the beginnings of the downfall of the Tory party.

**JUNE**      US President John F Kennedy gives his ground breaking, "Ich bin ein Berliner", speech offering American solidarity to the citizens of West Berlin.

**JULY**      Kim Philby is named as 'The Third Man' in the Burgess and Maclean spy ring and the Soviet newspaper Izvestia reports that the double agent has been given asylum in Moscow.

**AUGUST**      'The Great Train Robbery' on the travelling Post Office train from Glasgow to Euston, takes place in Buckinghamshire.

**SEPTEMBER**      Malaysia is formed through the merging of the Federation of Malaya and the British crown colony of Singapore, North Borneo and Sarawak.

**OCTOBER**      Harold Wilson resigns on grounds of ill health and Alec Douglas-Home succeeds him as Prime Minister of the UK.
The new National Theatre gives its first performance, with Peter O'Toole as Hamlet.

**NOVEMBER**      Malcolm X makes an historic speech in Detroit, Michigan. "Message to the Grass Roots"
John F Kennedy, the 35th president of the Unites States is assassinated in Dallas, Texas.
Lyndon B Johnson is sworn in as the new President.

**DECEMBER**      Zanzibar and Kenya gain independence from the United Kingdom and the Federation of Rhodesia and Nyasaland dissolves.

# FILMS AND ARTS

**Lawrence of Arabia** starring Peter O'Toole and Alec Guinness wins the Oscar for Best Picture.

The publicity of the affair between the stars, Elizabeth Taylor and Richard Burton, helped make **Cleopatra** a huge box office success but the film was a financial disaster.

New Films released included **Summer Holiday** starring Cliff Richard; **The Great Escape** with Steve McQueen and **Tom Jones** starring Albert Finney and Susannah York which went on to win the Best Picture at the 1964 Oscars.

The first **Leeds Piano Competition** is held and Michael Roll is the winner.

Authors CS Lewis and Aldous Huxley both die on 23 November but news of their deaths is overshadowed by the assassination of JFK.

Leonardo da Vinci's **Mona Lisa** is exhibited in the US for the first (and only) time. Over four weeks for a period of four weeks, it is viewed by over half a million people.

William Hartnell stars as the First Doctor in the first episode of **Dr Who**

# 1963 THE YEAR

Born in 1963, you were one of 53.6 million people living in Britain and your life expectancy *then* was 70 years. You were one of the 18.3 births per 1,000 population and you had a 2.2% chance of dying as an infant, a rapidly declining chance as this figure in 1950 was almost 31%.

You were at the beginning of an exciting era of individualism, young people had found their voice and were heard. It was the tentative beginning of the feminist movement, saw the growth in campaigns against nuclear weapons and the war in Vietnam and in America, the racial intolerance brought to the fore, civil rights leader Martin Luther King.

Mr. Edward Craven-Walker invented his psychedelic Astro (lava) lamp in 1963. The idea came from an egg-timer he saw in a Dorset pub that was made by a regular. Edward envisaged he could illuminate and heat a 'non-mixing' special coloured wax in a clear or translucent liquid to create a visual ornament.

## HOW MUCH DID IT COST?

| | | |
|---|---|---|
| The Average Pay: | £860 | (£17 p.w) |
| The Average House: | £3,160 | |
| Loaf of White Bread: | 1s 2½ d (6p) | |
| Pint of Milk: | 8½ d | (3p) |
| Pint of Beer: | 2s 1d | (10½p) |
| Dozen Eggs: | 4s | (20p) |
| Gallon of Petrol: | 4s 9d | (23p) 5p/litre |
| Newspapers: | 5d | (2p) |
| To post a letter in UK: | 3d | (1p) |
| Television licence | £5 (Black and White) | |

In 1963 the standard rate of income tax was 7s 9d in the pound (39%). American Express introduced the first credit cards into Britain and freeze-dried instant coffee was first introduced by Maxwell House. Every teenager owned a transistor radio and enjoyed BBC Radio 1. Dr Who and the Daleks were born and Weight Watchers started in the US.

## POPULAR MUSIC

The Beatles have three number 1's in the UK charts in their first year. **From Me to You, She Loves You** – which was also the year's best selling single - and **I Want to Hold Your Hand.** Their debut album, **Please Please Me,** reaches the top of the album charts.

First time top ten artists included Dusty Springfield, Gerry and the Pacemakers and The Searchers.

JANUARY - With 16 weeks in the Top Ten, **Telstar** by The Tornados, is still celebrating the satellite.

FEBRUARY - A melody used in the film, **Never on Sunday** was turned into a hit single recorded by Brenda Lee as **All Alone Am I**.

MAY - **Do You Want to Know a Secret** took Billy J Kramer to No 2 with his cover of the Beatles song sung by George Harrison.

JULY - The Searchers have the first of their two No 1's in the year with **Sweets For My Sweet** which stayed at the top for two consecutive weeks.

OCTOBER - Gerry and the Pacemakers become the very first act to reach number 1 with their first three singles. **How Do You Do It"** (April), **I Like It** (June) and **You'll Never Walk Alone** (Oct)

NOVEMBER - The Shadows had the most top 10 hits of the year with nine hit singles, four of which were with Cliff Richard, including this last of the year, **Don't Talk to Him**.

## THE START OF DR WHO

The show's launch was overshadowed by the assassination of John F Kennedy the previous day and so many people complained they had missed it because of programme rescheduling, that it was repeated the following week before Episode 2.

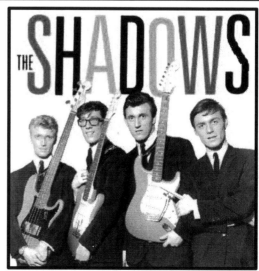

In 1968 there were no state pre-schools or nurseries, so for most children at five years old, the first day at school was the first time they would have spent the day away from family or friends and for most, because their mother would have been home with them all day, the first time they would be separated. But for the child, school life had a routine – calling the register, lessons, playtime and mid-morning, the mostly dreaded, 'school milk'. Warmed by the sun or worse, when frozen, warmed by the radiator!

Reading, writing and arithmetic were most important; times tables were learnt by rote as was poetry; neat handwriting was practiced daily, and nature study was 'science' with leaves and acorns being identified and then becoming 'arts and crafts'.

## CHILDREN'S TV

Aged five in 1968, when you were home from school, you could watch – in black and white of course, Pugh, Pugh and Barney Mcgrew, Cuthbert, Dibble and Grub in **Trumpton**, or if at five you were 'casting aside babyish things', **Magpie**, ITV's answer to BBC's **Blue Peter**. Everyone collected milk bottle tops and used stamps for the **Blue Peter** appeals and even at five, you probably went "out to play" in the street with your friends.

## HOW MUCH DID IT COST?

| | | |
|---|---|---|
| The Average Pay: | £890 | (£17 p.w) |
| The Average House: | £4,010 | |
| Loaf of White Bread: | 1s 4d | (7p) |
| Pint of Milk: | 10d | (4p) |
| Pint of Beer: | 2s 6d | (12.5p) |
| 12 months Road Tax | £25 | |
| Gallon of Petrol: | 6s 2d | (31p) |
| Newspapers: | 4d - 9d | (1.5p- 4p) |
| To post a letter in UK: | 5d | (2p) |
| TV Licence | £5 black & white | £10 Colour |

"Quick Brew is the third largest selling brand in both the Tea Bag and Packet Tea markets in the United Kingdom." *

*It was Tetley in 1953 that drove the introduction of tea bags in Britain, but other companies soon caught up. In the early 1960s, tea bags made up less than 3 per cent of the British market, but this has been growing steadily ever since. The key selling points were no tea leaves to dispose of and the fact that a tea pot was not needed - you could make the tea directly in the cup.*

## POPULAR MUSIC

1968 was a ground-breaking year for rock music. From the release of the Beatles' **White Album** to the formation of Led Zeppelin and the release of Jimi Hendrix's first album, **Are You Experienced**, it was a year that saw the genre change forever.

The Beatles had the best-selling single of the year with **Hey Jude**, written by Paul McCartney, and the first release on their 'Apple' label.

JANUARY The Christmas No1, **Hello Goodbye** by The Beatles, stayed at the top and the first new No1 was **The Ballad of Bonnie and Clyde** by Georgie Fame.

MARCH. **What a Wonderful World/Cabaret** was No1 for four weeks making Louis Armstrong at 66 the oldest artist to have a UK singles No1

JUNE Des O'Connor, often the butt of Morecambe & Wise comedy, had one of his four UK No1s with **I Pretend.**

JULY Simon & Garfunkel's **Mrs Robinson** from the film 'The Graduate' reached No4 in the charts. The song had been 'third choice' for the film.

SEPTEMBER 18 year-old Mary Hopkin spent six consecutive weeks at No1 with her debut single, **Those Were the Days.** The longest running No1 of the year.

DECEMBER The comedy group Scaffold released **Lily the Pink** - her medicinal compound with efficacious cures - stayed at the top of the charts for four weeks over the Christmas holidays.

# 1974 THE YEAR

1974 was a grim year for Britain economically, starting off with a 3-day week to conserve electricity, a 50mph speed limit on all roads and television was required to close down at 10.30 every evening. However, there was much to enjoy, the huge expansion of package holidays, particularly for destinations such as Torremolinos and Benidorm in Spain, meant families could forget their woes for a fortnight and enjoy the sun, sand and sangria. Abba won the Eurovision with **Waterloo** and all youngsters seemed to want to be Kung Fu fighting.

Package tours to sunny, warm and cheap holiday destinations were very popular. Companies such as Thompson, Horizon, Global and Clarksons all used chartered planes to fly families to booming resorts Once there, holiday makers found that in addition to the sun and sand, food and drink was much cheaper than in the UK and this led to the rapid decline in UK seaside resorts and boom in once sleepy fishing villages such as Benidorm.

Kentucky Fried Chicken and Wimpey Bars were already established in Britain and when MacDonald's, serving hamburgers and French fries opened their first restaurant in London in 1974, the trend was sealed for fast food. Eating became fun and fried food fast became a favourite. At home, the friendly Martians were encouraging everyone to eat Smash not Mash!

## LIFE AGE ELEVEN

Eleven year olds went from being the 'king-pins' at primary school to 'the newcomers', either at Grammar School if they'd passed the 11+ exam or Secondary Modern if not. It was the start of growing up but at home there was still plenty of fun. Chopper bikes were all the rage; space hoppers still 'cool' enough; playing fields still existed and there was colour TV. **Dr Who** could scare you and Roy Castle encourage you to be a **Record Breaker**.

## HOW MUCH DID IT COST?

| | |
|---|---|
| The Average Pay: | £2,500 (£48 p.w) |
| The Average House: | £10,000 |
| Loaf of White Bread: | 14p |
| Pint of Milk: | 4p |
| Pint of Beer: | 22p |
| Gallon of Petrol: | 50p |
| 12mnths Road Tax | £25 |
| Newspapers: | 43p - 8p |
| To post a letter in UK: | 4.5p |
| TV Licence | £7 Black & White £12 Colour |

## POPULAR MUSIC

ABBA, Eric Clapton, Queen and Showaddywaddy were among the artists who had their first UK No 1 hit. The 1973 Christmas No1, **Merry Christmas Everybody** by Slade stayed at the top for two weeks in January.

Mud had the best-selling single of the year with **Tiger Feet** which spent four weeks at No1 and the glam-rock group had three other top 10's including the Christmas No1, **Lonely This Christmas.**

FEBRUARY  The Wombles had four hits, **Wombling Song** No4, **Remember You're a Womble**, No3, **Banana Rock** No9 and **Wombling Merry Christmas** No2.

*Popular TV programmes included: Are You Being Served?, The Benny Hill Show, Colditz, Dad's Army, and Doctor Who. The main soaps were Emmerdale (started 1972) and Coronation Street (1960). Radio's The Archers had started in 1951.*

MARCH Paper Lace had the first of two top-ten singles this year with **Billy Don't Be a Hero**. It stayed at No1 for three weeks.

JUNE Charles Aznavour wrote **She** in English as the theme song for the TV series 'Seven Faces of Woman' and it became his only UK No1.

JULY The first Knebworth open air, rock and pop concert is held in England. Headlined by The Allman Brothers Band and the Doobie Brothers, only 60,000 fans attended.

NOVEMBER **Gonna Make You a Star,** was the first No1 for David Essex and the first of many top forty hits made by the singer who combined singing with an extensive acting career.

DECEMBER Barry White had two weeks at the top before Christmas with **You're the First, the Last, My Everything.**

# 1979 THE YEAR

In the Trade Union battles of 1979, while the gravediggers were on strike and towns piled high with uncollected rubbish, popular culture and alcohol could bring relief. It was the age of lager. Carling Black Label, Skol and Harp were challenging Watney's Red Barrel and Party Seven to be the idea of drinking. Wine was popular too, Blue Nun and Tower, the sweet German wines, and of course, Mateus Rosé, the slightly fizzy pink wine in the bottle that often ended up as the base for a lamp. However, the 70s would never have been complete without Martini "Any time, any place, anywhere".

TV was the family's main entertainment. British favourites 'Are You Being Served' and 'Last of the Summer Wine' were joined by glamorous American imports, 'Dallas' and 'Charlie's Angels' whilst at the cinema, when you were sixteen, you could watch all but the X rated films.

## LIFE AT SIXTEEN

Sixteen in 1979, you could leave school; could join the army; legally buy cigarettes as well as smoke them; pubs were only open lunchtimes and evenings, but you couldn't have a beer unless an "adult" over 18 had bought it for you and you were eating a meal.

Long hair and flared trousers were de rigueur for boys and girls, Curly Wurly's were a favourite snack along with Topic Bars, Marathons and Bounty - the 'taste of tropical paradise'

## HOW MUCH DID IT COST?

| | |
|---|---|
| The Average Pay: | £5,250 (£101 p.w) |
| The Average House: | £19,925 |
| Loaf of White Bread: | 26p |
| Pint of Milk: | 15p |
| Pint of Beer: | 34p |
| 12mnths Road Tax | £50 |
| Gallon of Petrol: | 98p |
| Newspapers: | 8p - 15p |
| To post a letter in UK: | 10p |
| TV Licence | £12 Black & White £34 Colour |

# You Were Sixteen

## Popular Music

Art Garfunkel had the best-selling single of 1979 with **Bright Eyes** from the soundtrack of the film 'Watership Down'. It stayed at No1 for six weeks and another soundtrack from a film **Cavatina, The Deer Hunter** by The Shadows reached No9.

**Heart of Glass** and **Sunday Girl** both became No1s for Blondie whilst **Dreaming** made No2, all three included in the year's top 10 best-sellers.

JANUARY The crowd-pleasing **YMCA** by The Village People was the first new No 1 of the year.

FEBRUARY Frequently recalled as a symbol of female empowerment, **I Will Survive** reached the top for Gloria Gaynor.

MAY **Dance Away** by the rock band Roxy Music was written by Bryan Ferry and although only managing second place in the charts, it became the ninth biggest selling single in the UK in 1979 and one of their best-known songs.

AUGUST Cliff Richard had his first No1 in eleven years with **We Don't Talk Anymore** which stayed four weeks at the top and was the third best-selling single of the year.

OCTOBER **When You're in Love with a Beautiful Woman** by Dr Hook was No1. The song first appeared on the band's 1978 album **Pleasure and Pain**.

*Margaret Thatcher opened the new Central Milton Keynes Shopping Centre, the largest indoor shopping centre in Britain.*

DECEMBER The Wall, Pink Floyd's rock opera was released featuring all three parts of **Another Brick in the Wall. Part 2**, written as a protest against rigid schooling.

'Do They Know It's Christmas?'

It may have been the year of the miners' strike but there was still much to celebrate during the year. Torvill and Dean won a gold medal at the Winter Olympics, skating to Ravel's **'Bolero'**; Lloyd Webber's roller-skating extravaganza, **'Starlight Express'** opened in London; ITV showed the first episode of the gritty police drama, **'The Bill'** and at the end of the year, 36 of Britain and Ireland's top pop musicians formed Band Aid and recorded the song **Do They Know It's Christmas** to raise money for famine relief in Ethiopia.

## THE DIGITAL AGE ARRIVES

Twenty-one in 1984, you were at the forefront of the world of personal computers and Apple launched their first Apple Mackintosh this year. The Mac included MacPaint and MacWrite, which demonstrated WYSIWYG (What You See Is What You Get) word processing.

Take home a Macintosh.
No purchase necessary.

Test drive a Macintosh.

Phillips introduced the CD-ROM which led to multimedia encyclopaedias, games, novels and reference information on CD and Fujio Masuoka invented flash memory, capable of being erased and re-programmed multiple times.

Fashion had moved away from the 70s styles and pop stars like Cyndi Lauper were bringing in an entirely new look, especially for the young. Brightly coloured accessories like sunglasses, bangles and hoop earrings were a necessity. Teased hair, loud makeup and neon were all important.

## HOW MUCH DID IT COST?

| | |
|---|---|
| The Average Pay: | £8,008  (£154p.w) |
| The Average House: | £30,100 |
| Loaf of White Bread: | 38p |
| Pint of Milk: | 21p |
| Pint of Beer: | 66p |
| 12mnths Road Tax | £90 |
| Gallon of Petrol: | £1.87 |
| Newspapers: | 16p - 20p |
| To post a letter in UK: | 17p |
| TV Licence | £15 Black & White £46 Colour |

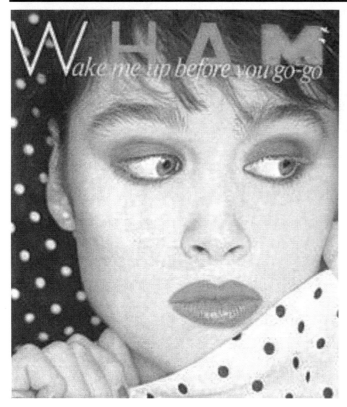

## POPULAR MUSIC

George Michael had five top tens. These included two No1s with his group Wham! **Wake Me Up Before You Go-Go** and **Freedom**, plus his No1 solo hit **Careless Whisper**. He also sang in the year's best selling single, **Do They Know It's Christmas** by Band Aid.

Frankie Goes to Hollywood reached No1 in January with their debut single **Relax,** but the record was banned by the BBC because of its doubtful lyrics.

JUNE **Heaven Knows I'm Miserable Now** was the first top ten entry for The Smiths – it got to No10.

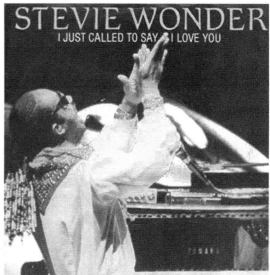

FEBRUARY **Girls Just Want to Have Fun** took Cyndi Lauper to No2, the first time in the top ten in the UK and **Time After Time** took the third spot in June.

APRIL Simon Le Bon and Duran Duran had four top ten hits this year and was No1 for four weeks with **The Reflex.**

AUGUST Stevie Wonder had six weeks at No1 with **I Just Called to Say I Love You** which featured in the film 'The Woman in Red'.

OCTOBER Philip Oakey was the lead singer in The Human League and he collaborated with Giorgio Moroder for **Together in Electric Dreams,** for the film 'Electric Dreams', and it was his first single in the top ten in his own right.

The VW Golf GTI was the ultimate hot hatchback of the time, and one in which all self-respecting yuppies hoped they'd be starting their driving career.

DECEMBER Paul McCartney joined with the Frog Chorus in the 'Rupert' film and **We All Stand Together** reached No3 in the charts.

## SPORTING HEADLINES

JANUARY The third round of the **FA Cup** began and lasted 66 days through frost, snow, ice, power cuts, thaw, rain and mud. It was spread over 22 different playing days and there were 261 postponements. Sixteen of the 32 ties were called off 10 or more times.

MARCH In **Rugby Union,** England won the Five Nations Championship.

Mill House, at 18 hands, known as 'The Big Horse', wins the **Cheltenham Gold Cup.**

APRIL Jack Nicklaus was the then-youngest winner of the **Masters Tournament** at Augusta, Georgia. He went on to win the **PGA Championship** in just his second year as a professional.

Manchester Utd vs Leicester City
1963 FA Cup Final

MAY In the **FA Cup Final,** Manchester United beat Leicester City 3-1. The match was played at Wembley Stadium which was fully roofed for the first time.

JUNE The **Tour de France** was won by Jacques Anquetil, the Frenchman was the first to win the Tour five times, in 1957 and from 1961 to 1964.

JULY Tennis on the final Saturday at **Wimbledon** was cancelled due to rain and the ladies' singles final was held on the Monday. No1 seed, Margaret Smith defeated unseeded Billie Jean Moffitt to win the title.

A RINGSIDE SEAT AT *EVERY* FIGHT

BOXING NEWS

World's Premier Fight Wee[k]

Vol. 19   No. 30   54th Year     PRICE NINEPENCE

LISTON WINS — I[N] 130 SECS.!

The **Boxing Heavyweight Championship** of the world was won by Sonny Liston. He knocked out Floyd Patterson in the first round of the fight in Las Vegas, a repeat of the previous year when he gained the title after knocking Patterson out in the first round also.

SEPTEMBER Limited Overs **Cricket**, one day cricket, began in 1963 with the first edition of the knockout competition, the **Gillette Cup,** won by Sussex. The hundredth edition of Wisden's Almanack was published.

OCTOBER The 'All Blacks' **Rugby** team toured Britain and Ireland where their only loss was in October to Newport RFC, but the New Zealanders were deprived of a Grand Slam by a scoreless draw with Scotland.

DECEMBER Jim Clark won his first **Formula One Championship** driving a Lotus-Climax. In the ten races, he had seven wins to two by Graham Hill and one by John Surtees. *This record number of wins in a season was not beaten until 1988 by Ayrton Senna.*

# SPORTING EVENTS

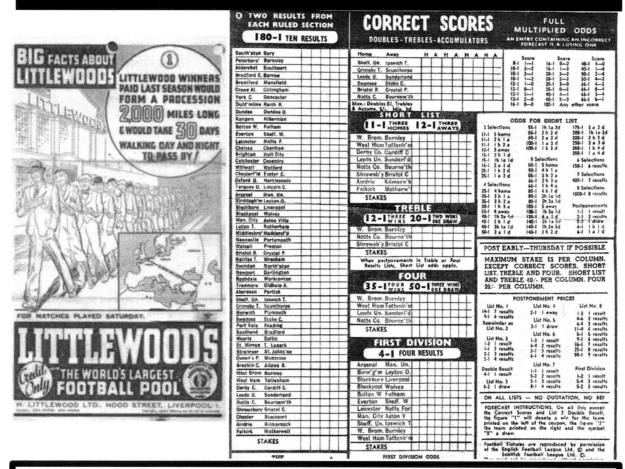

## THE POOLS PANEL IS BORN

Freezing fog enveloped Britain just a few days before Christmas 1962 and by Boxing Day, arctic winds and snow had swept the country and was to remain on the ground for the best part of three months. The country was brought to a standstill along with all the sporting fixtures and although five third-round FA Cup ties went ahead on 5 January, the round wasn't completed until 11 March.

The draw for the FA Cup was chaotic, the fixtures being drawn for each round despite many games being left incomplete as the wait for pitches to thaw out dragged on. In 1963, Football Pools were very popular. They were a 'betting pool' for predicting the outcome of top-level football matches taking place in the coming week. It was typically cheap to play, and entries were sent in, to Littlewoods or Vernons, through the post, or via agents who collected the 'coupons' and cash from your door. The most popular game was the Treble Chance where you had to predict the matches to end in a 'draw'.

The lack of matches wreaked havoc for the lucrative football pools empires and disappointment for their thousands of customers, so the companies needed to do something quickly. By the end of January, a predictions system was put in place where postponed or cancelled matches were judged on by a panel of experts and the punters could still be in with a chance to win. The 'Pools Panel' sat for the first time on 23 January, the six-man panel comprised former top-level players and referees. Their deliberations were made behind closed doors in London, and they predicted 7 draws, 8 away victories and 23 home victories, these being announced live on BBC television. Of the 38 matches, the only predictions to raise eyebrows were Peterborough to beat Derby and Leeds to beat Stoke.

17

# 1963

## Elizabeth Plays Cleopatra Opposite Burton

Elizabeth Taylor and Richard Burton began their love affair while filming **Cleopatra**. Paparazzi photographs of the couple appeared in all the papers and their 'on' 'off' scandal caught the public's imagination and provided a huge amount of free publicity. **Cleopatra** was the most expensive film ever to be released, the original budget of $2 million had swollen to $44 million. There were 30 wigs for Cleopatra and 125 pieces of jewellery; the extra's in the battle scenes had 26,000 costumes that cost half a million dollars, palm trees were flown in from California, a fanciful barge cost $250,000 plus exotic animals, and a dress made from 24-carat gold thread. The result was that although the film won Oscars for costume design, cinematography, production design and best visual effects, it proved to be a financial disaster.

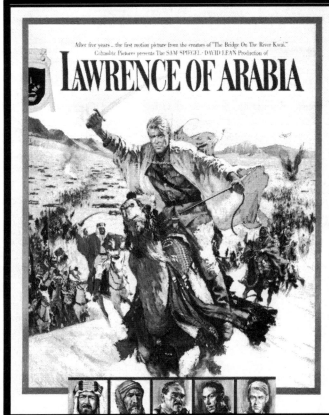

## Seven Oscars For Lawrence Of Arabia

*If you are the man with the money and somebody comes to you and says he wants to make a film that's four hours long, with no stars, and no women, and no love story, and not much action either, and he wants to spend a huge amount of money to film it in the desert – what would you say?*
– Omar Sharif on **Lawrence of Arabia**

The epic drama of TE Lawrence, the English officer who successfully united and led the diverse, often warring, Arab tribes during World War I in order to fight the Turks had an "all-star" cast. Peter O'Toole played Lawrence, Alec Guinness, Prince Faisal and Omar Sharif, Sherif Ali. David Lean's film was nominated for ten Oscars and won seven, including Best Picture and Best Director.

# CULTURAL EVENTS

## MONA LISA VISITS NEW YORK

Leonardo da Vinci's masterpiece, the **Mona Lisa** was on show this year for the first, *(and only)* time in America at the National Gallery of Art in Washington DC. Thanks to the efforts of Jackie Kennedy it was the first time the work had left the Louvre in 50 years, having been stolen previously by an Italian nationalist. Over 2,000 dignitaries, including the President viewed the painting on the first night and the next day, the exhibit opened to the public. 500,000 people went to see this portrait of the wife of a wealthy Florentine citizen, Francesco del Gioconda, painted in 1504. 'La Gioconda' is famous for her enigmatic expression, both aloof and alluring. She went on to 'smile' at a further million people in New York's Metropolitan Museum of Art.

with the beatles                    stereo

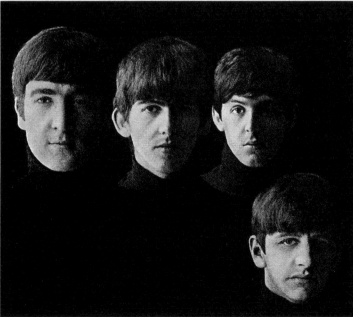

## SCREAMING GIRLS CATCH BEATLE MANIA

In 1963, the Beatles had three number 1's in the UK charts, **From Me to You, She Loves You** and **I Want to Hold Your Hand.** Their debut album, **Please Please Me**, reached the top of the album charts within four weeks of being released and it remained in that position for 30 weeks. Their second album **With the Beatles** followed in the autumn becoming their first million-selling album, and the second album of any kind in Britain to sell one million copies, the first being the **South Pacific** soundtrack.

'Beatle Mania' had broken out all over the country and the 'Fab Four's' appearances were met by throngs of screaming girls. They performed at 257 concerts and by the end of the year, were poised to take America by storm.

# 1963

## MODERN TRANSPLANTS

1963 saw great progress in the medical world, with Thomas Starzl, an American physician, performing the very first human liver transplant at the University of Colorado. His success was constrained because of the ineffective immuno-suppressive drugs used and the patient did not live for more than a couple of weeks

Although kidney transplants began in 1950, it was in 1963 that Guy Alexandre, a Belgian doctor was the first to take kidneys from brain-dead donors which, although many of his colleagues considered this ethically unacceptable at the time, was a major advance in organ transplantation.

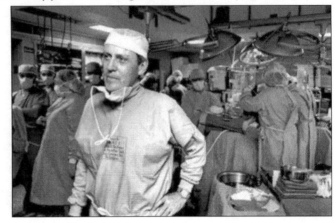

Another American doctor, James D Harvey, carried out the first lung transplant at the University of Mississippi, with his patient living for 18 days. Hardy also performed the world's first modern heart transplant attempt the following year when he transplanted the heart of a chimpanzee into a dying man. The heart beat for approximately one hour.

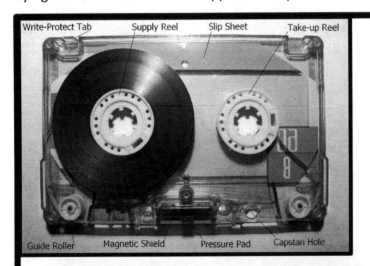

Write-Protect Tab    Supply Reel    Slip Sheet    Take-up Reel

Guide Roller    Magnetic Shield    Pressure Pad    Capstan Hole

### Cassette Tape

The cassette tape had been developed by Philips in Belgium in 1962 but it was not realised to the world until 1963. These two small spools inside its plastic case, which wind magnetic-coated film and pass it from one side to the other, meant music could now be recorded and shared by everyone.

Not only could you record your favourite songs, but you could create your own mixed tapes and not just for yourself. Taking the time to compile and record selected tracks showed true devotion for a friend or sweetheart! However, the original purpose of the compact cassette tape was for dictation, but it was the passion to use it for music that led to more than 3 billion tapes being sold over its lifetime from 1963 until 1988.

## THE INSTAMATIC

Kodak introduced their Instamatic camera in 1963. The name came from the way in which the film was loaded, quite simply and instantly, a film cartridge was inserted into the camera and it was ready to shoot. Amateur photographers found it very easy, the cameras were inexpensive and the first to use Kodak's new 126 format. The easy-load film cartridge made them inexpensive to produce, as it provided the backing plate and exposure counter itself, making an easy design and lower manufacturing costs.

The Instamatic was an instant success and heralded a generation of cheap photography, the line being sold from 1963 up to 1988 with over 5 million cameras being produced and sold in the first 7 years. The instamatic name is still used to describe any inexpensive point and shoot Kodak camera on the market.

## SKOPJE EARTHQUAKE

In July an earthquake hit Skopje, then in Yugoslavia - now Macedonia - resulting in 1,100 deaths and some 4,000 people injured. It made headlines around the world and the story captured public attention, partly because it was one of the first disasters to attract massive TV coverage. Nearly 80 countries offered relief supplies and humanitarian considerations outweighed political differences as the USA was in the forefront of the relief effort, quickly flying in a mobile field hospital to care for the injured.

Skopje's partially ruined old railway station is now the city museum, the large dock on the street elevation has not been touched since it stopped at 17.17, the precise moment when the earthquake struck.

European style had already begun to dominate the fashion world and whilst, for older people, the look in 1963 was still reminiscent of the 50's - conservative and restrained, the American First Lady, Jackie Kennedy, had a huge influence on a whole generation. She wore elegant outfits, suits and simple yet stylish shift dresses in block colours. She paired these with the pill box hats she popularised, button earrings and white gloves and embraced the bouffant hairstyle which, with the help of Audrey Hepburn and Brigitte Bardot, developed into the iconic 'beehive.'

Young men were influenced by the Beatles, who moved away from leather jackets, polo necks and cowboy boots to the grey 'collarless' suit which became the most iconic of Beatle looks. It was usually worn by the fab four in grey but also made several appearances in black and not to forget, mop top hair, made famous by the Fab Four and imitated around the country.

As a child you could spend your pocket money, probably still about 6d a week, on your favourite sweet treats. Rolls of Love Hearts were put in their special Christmas Crackers by Swizzels. They were such a success that the fizzy sweets with their fun messages became permanent, selling at 3d a pack.

One of the best sweets for sharing were Rowntree's Fruit Gums. Their famous slogan: "Don't forget the Fruit Gums, Mum" was changed to "Chum", not "Mum" in 1961 when the company became aware of accusations of 'pester power' and didn't want the nation's mothers disapproving of them as a brand.

Treets, Peanut, Toffee or Chocolate, which 'Melt in your mouth, not in your hand', and more and more sweets in packets rather than being weighed out by the shopkeeper from jars and handed over in little paper bags.

## BUTLIN'S HOLIDAY CAMP SKEGNESS
### IT'S QUICKER BY RAIL

Your holiday during the 6 week summer break was likely to be in Britain. Holiday camps such as Butlins with their 'Red Coats' offered hours of fun, coaches could take you to the seaside and owning a caravan was becoming popular too.

In 1963 the nuclear family was still the norm, father out at work and mother busy with the housework which was time consuming before the general possession of electrical labour-saving devices. Washing up was done by hand and laundry gradually moved to machines over the decade. Twin tubs, one for washing and one for spinning, became popular in the late 60's and were usually wheeled into the kitchen to be attached to the cold tap and afterwards, have the waste-water emptied into the sink. The 'housewife' had to be at home to transfer the wet washing from the washing tub to the spinning tub.

Goods came to you. The milkman delivered the milk to your doorstep, the baker brought the baskets of bread to the door, the greengrocer delivered and the 'pop man' came once a week with 'dandelion and burdock', 'cherryade' or 'cream soda' and the rag and bone man visited the street for your recycling.

# JANUARY 1ST - 7TH 1963

## IN THE NEWS

**Tuesday 1**    **"New Year Tonic"** The Chancellor of the Exchequer reduced purchase tax on television sets, radios, gramophones and records, perfumery and cosmetics from 45 per cent to 25 per cent.

**Wednesday 2**    **"Worst Snow for 82 Years"** The Met Office forecast more blizzards to come and the West Country, already cut off from the rest of Britain by blocked roads, is threatened again.

**Thursday 3**    **"It Thaws! It Freezes!"** As Britain's blizzard swept North, a new menace hit the south, a 'freezing' thaw which formed black ice on many roads.

**Friday 4**    **"Power Cuts in London"** A blackout in some parts of London and Essex was the first big effect of the unofficial work-to-rule campaign and overtime ban by electricity supply workers. Further stoppages threatened as pay talks fail.

**Saturday 5**    **"Fire Cripples P&O Liner"** Fire struck the 45,000-ton liner Canberra, flagship of the P&O Lines fleet, as she steamed off the southern tip of Italy.

**Sunday 6**    **"Now the Hazard is Potholes"** Road conditions throughout most of the country moved very slowly towards getting back to normal, but the number of roads already cracked or potholed, some over six inches deep, are now adding to the motorists' difficulties.

**Monday 7**    **"Angry Passengers Refuse Air Lift"** On board the fire-crippled Canberra, 300 held a meeting to demand that P&O arrange for them to continue their journey to Australia in a liner of comparable comfort.

## HERE IN BRITAIN

### "Snob Value Phones"

The Post Office charges 30s extra to install a coloured phone, but all phones cost £6 to make, exactly the same as the ordinary black ones which are put in free. The Post-Master General was asked about this 'snob tax' in the Commons and told his questioner, (owner of a two-tone grey) he would "look into it"!

When coloured telephones were first introduced in 1956, they cost £5 to install. A spokesman said, "We cannot have people changing their minds about the colour on a whim or a fancy – we would have piles of black phones on the scrapheap!"

## AROUND THE WORLD

### "BAOR Brawling Again"

British soldiers have been involved in another fight in Minden, West Germany, which was the scene of serious brawls last summer. This time it involved men of the Worcester Regiment who fought amongst themselves in a pub two miles outside the town.

When a German civilian stepped in to try and stop them, he was punched, and three soldiers are now under arrest. Minden is the town where the Cameronians (Scottish Rifles) earned the nickname "Poison Dwarfs" because of their frequent and aggressive fighting with civilians, which ultimately led to a series of courts martial and a high-level Army inquiry.

# THE CANBERRA CATCHES FIRE

Fire struck the 45,000-ton liner Canberra, flagship of the P&O Orient Lines fleet, as she steamed eastwards off the southern tip of Italy. The main engines were put out of action and the £16m liner, Britain's biggest to be built since the Queen Elizabeth, came to a standstill. Luckily the fire, in the main engine room switchboard, was brought under control within an hour and there were no casualties and she managed to reach Valletta in Malta where she could be repaired.

The Canberra was four days out of Southampton bound for Australia and the Pacific. The biggest and costliest liner built in Britain since the war, the Canberra has been plagued by repeated mechanical failures since she left Harland and Wolff's shipyard in Belfast in the spring of 1961. After growing labour troubles during the final months of construction she left the yard with much work still to be done and had engine trouble during her sea trials.

On her maiden voyage she arrived in Australia a day late after a condenser fault which affected her air conditioning. On her second voyage she broke a turbine blade on leaving Colombo and arrived back in England five days late for dry docking and boiler cleaning. Last spring she was brought back early from a round-the-world voyage and spent a month in dry dock, since when she has had no trouble until this week.

The chairman of P&O said, *"The Canberra is a revolutionary ship. With her superb lido, comfortable cabins and brilliant decor, she has been an immediate success with passengers and has been heavily booked. But her huge turbo-electric engines and complicated auxiliaries have been less successful and there is no doubt that so far she has certainly been a headache to operate."*

# JANUARY 8ᵀᴴ - 14ᵀᴴ 1963

## IN THE NEWS

**Tuesday 8**  "Severe Frosts to Continue" An increasing easterly wind brought very cold air from the Continent and the temperature stayed below freezing all day in many parts of southern and central England.

**Wednesday 9**  "Electrical Trades Union Ban on Overtime" Unofficial action, in support of their pay claim, spread to the Midlands and the North. 30,000 members in the electricity supply industry were ordered to stop working overtime.

**Thursday 10**  "More Cash for BBC Actors" An agreement signed by the BBC and Equity after nine months of negotiations, provides a new fee structure based on the length of programme and on the length of the artist's engagement.

**Friday 11**  "Air Lines Hope to Avoid Fares War" Agreement on Economy class fares was reached with 18 members of the International Air Transport Association operating DC 7C (propeller driven) airliners between New York and Scandinavia.

**Saturday 12**  "Move to Raise Criminal Age to 10" The Government propose to raise the age of criminal responsibility from eight years to 10 by an amendment to the Children and Young Persons Bill.

**Sunday 13**  "Blazing Train in Tunnel" Seventy passengers scrambled to safety when the 7.30pm York to Liverpool diesel train caught fire as it entered a half-mile tunnel, two minutes after stopping at Sowerby Bridge.

**Monday 14**  "Army NCOs Take Over in Togo" Military insurgents in the West African state assassinated President Olympio, shooting him down two yards from the gate of the US Embassy, where he was going to seek refuge.

## HERE IN BRITAIN

### "They're No Dummies"

Two dummy figures displaying clothes in a West End shop window were removed after it was found that they resembled the Duke of Edinburgh and President Kennedy. An official of Montague Burton (Tailors) said, "The two dummies had been in the window for about six months, and we had no idea.

They are made by Jacques Bodart of Gems, who tells us that he takes interesting and striking looking types of face for his models. He made about 150 of these dummies and we have bought six, so there must be a lot of them in other shop windows."

## AROUND THE WORLD

### "Parisian Pigeon Fanciers"

Protests by Parisian bird-lovers against the ban on feeding pigeons in public places have led the Prefect of Police to reassure a member of the municipal council that the ban will not become effective until enough lofts have been installed to provide home comforts and food for the pigeons. Many people are seen daily scattering on the pavements, enough bread and titbits to last even the hungriest pigeons a week. The authorities probably went too far for the tender-hearted in distributing warning posters showing bandaged pigeons facing execution squads if the feeding did not stop.

# BRITAIN'S BIG FREEZE

The Big Freeze plus the power workers 'go slow', produced unprecedented travel chaos. But there were some less publicised effects of the weather too.

Thousands of gallons of milk were thrown away on isolated dairy farms. Milk and bread was delivered by helicopter. Stranded coach passengers were rescued by helicopter. Salt stocks ran out leaving authorities with none to clear snowbound streets. The Freeze sent the price of vegetables and meat soaring. Cracks and potholes formed in roads, some over six inches deep. More than 1,500 sheep, cattle and Dartmoor ponies needed to be rescued and fed. Hexworthy on Dartmoor were without newspapers for a fortnight and Christmas holidaymakers were stranded there until the middle of January. An avalanche blocked the main railway line between Edinburgh station and Carlisle, and a shepherd and his wife were weather bound at the top of the Lammermuir Hills for 16 days. Saturday 12th was a bad day for Soccer, 41 out of 46 League games were cancelled and the Pools stopped for three weeks. Horse racing was off and even rugby. Sugar beet processing factories in Norfolk closed for lack of beets, they were still in the ground.

An electricity chief pleaded *'put off Monday wash day to later in the week'* as the 'go slow' plus the Freeze caused power cuts for thousands. At Torquay and Herne Bay sea water froze. At a fire in Chester, firemen had to *start* a fire, over a frozen hydrant to get a water supply. Lifeboatmen at Walton were unable to reach their boat moored near the pier, the first time in 40 years. Lorry drivers lit small fires to thaw out their frozen diesel fuel systems. In a village in Kent, the beer froze in bottles at the White Swan and the infant's class of the school had their lessons in the Headmistress's dining room.

# JANUARY 15TH - 21ST 1963

## IN THE NEWS

**Tuesday 15**    **"De Gaulle Says Britain Not Ready"** The President held out small hope for Britain's entry into the Common Market, at least in the foreseeable future.

**Wednesday 16**    **"Mobile Rhine Army?"** Proposed changes in the role and organisation of the BAOR into a highly mobile force available to be moved quickly, would save ££ millions on equipment.

**Thursday 17**    **"Big Black Out in South-east"** Due to "massive disconnections" of the electricity supply, and very cold weather continuing to cause rising demands for power, parts of London and the south-east were blacked out for 2-3 hours.

**Friday 18**    **"Labour Leader Hugh Gaitskell Dies"** The leader of the Labour party, Hugh Gaitskell, died after a sudden deterioration in his heart condition.

**Saturday 19**    **"Common Market Decision Put Off"** An even stronger resistance to France's demands to suspend the negotiations for British entry into the EEC was put by the five other countries of the Community. The Six agreed to discuss the future of the negotiations again on January 28.

**Sunday 20**    **"Helicopters to the Rescue"** 283 civilian women who had been cut off for days by snow drifts at the Fylingdales early warning radar station in Yorkshire, were rescued by helicopter in one of the biggest airlifts to take place in Britain.

**Monday 21**    **"Emergency Bed Service Warns Hospitals"** The cold spell has thrown an extra burden on London's hospital beds. They are now dealing with 1,600 admissions a week and have issued a 'yellow card' warning to cut down on routine admissions.

## HERE IN BRITAIN

### "Parents Should Say 'No'"

The Home Secretary said this week that the level of crime and delinquency *"has grown so high that it is a disgrace to Britain, and the whole nation should feel the shame of it"*.

He regarded juvenile delinquency as the most important problem and *"If parents were to say 'No' to their children sometimes and not always give in to them, letting them grow up thinking they can do just what they like when they like, to whom they like, you will start emptying the juvenile courts. This would be an enormous step forward in the advance against adult crime."*

## AROUND THE WORLD

### "Masterpieces Used In Protests "

Rioting and an exchange of fire in which at least three persons were wounded, broke out in the grounds of the Central University in Caracas, Venezuela when heavily armed troops began to search the university buildings for five French impressionist paintings stolen by an armed gang from the city's Museum. A member of the gang had told onlookers that the paintings would be displayed at a left-wing political meeting to draw attention to its fight against President Betancourt's Government and would later be returned. The paintings by Cezanne, Van Gogh, Picasso and Gaugin and Braque were recovered a week later.

# FORTS FOR SALE

For anyone who feels that an Englishman's home should really be a castle but who cannot afford a genuine Norman stronghold or even a medium size manor house with moat, the War Department are offering the next best thing by putting up for sale, six sea forts, four in the Solent and two at the mouth of the Humber. The Solent forts, which lie between Spit Sand at the entrance to Portsmouth harbour and St. Helen's Point on the Isle of Wight, were built between 1861 and 1880 because it was felt that the advent of the steamship posed dangers against which the Fleet was not sufficient security. Those in the Humber were built just before the First World War, and all six were manned throughout both world wars. Today their strategic potential has been deemed surplus to requirement and attempts will be made to sell them off individually.

To what extent a granite, concrete and armour-plated structure, even if it does possess some 40 rooms and is capable of accommodating over 100 men, can be described as a desirable residence is something the War Department are clearly in two minds about. Their spokesman admitted that the forts were not the sort of properties that lent themselves easily to modern living but at least their solid construction had in the past kept down maintenance costs. The War Department reckon to spend only £1,500 a year on the upkeep of all six forts, of which a large proportion goes on providing battery powered lights which serve as fixes for navigators. This service would probably have to be maintained by anyone who bought one of the forts - a small price to pay, one might argue, for a residence capable of withstanding anything short of a full-scale naval bombardment.

# JANUARY 22ND - 28TH 1963

## IN THE NEWS

**Tuesday 22**    **"Mr Macmillan's Bold Reply"** *"What had happened in the Common Market discussions had been a setback"*, he admitted to General de Gaulle, *"but we believe that we can be loyal Europeans without disloyalty to our great Commonwealth tradition and duty"*.

**Wednesday 23**    **"Ban on Use of Gas"** The South-western Gas Board issued a directive that gas must not be used between 9pm and 6am and between 2pm and 6pm. Wales Gas Board cut supplies to industry and hundreds of workers were sent home.

**Thursday 24**    **"Increases in Social Benefits"** An extra '10 bob' a week for pensioners, the sick and the unemployed at an initial cost of £227m.

**Friday 25**    **"Walking on Water"** For the first time this century people have been walking on the Thames above Windsor Bridge. The river was frozen for 100 yards from the Windsor bank to Eton College boat houses.

**Saturday 26**    **"£1 a Week Rise for Teachers"** Disappointed primary and secondary school teachers had their claim for a £4 a week pay rise rejected. £1 is an increase of just over 3% for 272,000 teachers.

**Sunday 27**    **"Continent Still in Grip of Cold Weather"** Europe is still in the grip of snow and ice. Road and rail traffic has been badly affected with power cuts and fuel shortages in many countries.

**Monday 28**    **"Weekend Thaw"** In Britain, the National Coal Board took advantage of a weekend thaw to mount a massive coal lift of 300,000 – 500,000 tons, throughout Britain.

## HERE IN BRITAIN

### "Clear That Snow"

A ratepayer made the first successful application for Barnes Borough Council to remove a 2ft pile of snow which he said was obstructing the roadway outside his home. Made under the 1959 Highways Act, which says that a highway authority must, if notice of an obstruction of snow is served, remove it within 24 hours or pay a fine of £5, the win opens the way for another 13,500 people in the borough. The applicant said, "There are side roads still completely blocked but 10 council men spent 1.5 hours clearing Barnes pond of lumps of ice and then watering the surface to improve it for skaters."

## AROUND THE WORLD

### "Bowled Over by The Champ"

The harmless looking game of boules led 15 men to be charged in Marseille with conspiracy to win 600,000 francs (over £40,000) from 25 different players. An aged and eccentric 'millionaire' approached builders who then arranged to meet their 'future client' – invariably playing boules and 'losing' thousands of francs to his opponents and to a crowd of alleged accomplices. To humour the old man, the victims joined in, winning at first, but when they got to the high stakes, the old man adjusted his sights and played like the champion he was, cleaning the board as well as his victims' pockets.

# YOUR COUNTRY NEEDS YOU

THE ARMY OF TODAY'S

ALL RIGHT!

This is the Army:
## THE LIFE FOR A MAN OF ACTION

Army Outward Bound School 1963

The War Office is launching a publicity campaign to improve the 'public image' of the Army officer. Young officers were questioned about why they joined, and at schools, headmasters were asked to discover what aspects of service life were least attractive to young men. They wish to build up a new and impressive picture of the military profession with the adverts showing the variety of experience and responsibility which face a young officer and the technical and academic challenges of service life.

Previous advertising has concentrated on the life of the Sandhurst cadet and it is clear that in the minds of many people, the profession consists principally of mentally enclosed buffoons who converse in sharp monosyllables and live exclusively on a diet of port. This is partly a result of some of the curiously stylised portraits which appear in certain television programmes where Army officers tend to wear their badges of rank upside down and get old-fashioned 'swagger sticks' caught between their legs. While the War Office do not deny that there are still officers whose intellectual gifts are minimal, in general the requirement for intelligence, enterprise and professional competence compares favourably with those of other professions.

At the same time, a symbol is needed to identify this new Army. The Navy's aircraft carrier and the V bombers of the Royal Air Force are vivid images, but for the Army, tanks, rifles and bayonets, however modern, are too evocative of past wars. The first advertisement carries a picture of a member of the Army's Outward Bound School negotiating a precipice in North Wales; it also carries the information that one of the attractions of the school is a *'6.45 am dip in the Irish Sea every morning'* - a prospect which many officers think is carrying image-making a shade too far.

# JAN 29TH - FEB 4TH 1963

## IN THE NEWS

**Tuesday 29** — "Two Killed in Soho Gun Fight" 'Tony the Greek' staggered out of his Dean Street club, The Grill, with head wounds and collapsed together with his doorman.

**Wednesday 30** — "Collapse of Brussels Talks" British entry to the EEC has been thwarted by one man. General de Gaulle has finally sabotaged the country's efforts to join in 1963.

**Thursday 31** — "Polaris Submarines" Mr Macmillan gave additional details on the Nassau agreement. Although it has not yet been decided what version of the missile will be ordered for British nuclear submarines, there will be four or five Polaris subs.

**Friday 1 Feb** — "Snowstorms Delay the Queen" The Queen and the Duke of Edinburgh, flying across Canada on their way to Fiji, made an unscheduled landing at Edmonton after snowstorms hit Vancouver airport, their first refuelling stop.

**Saturday 2** — "Berlin Escape on High Wire" A 36-year-old east German acrobat, Horst Klein, has fled to west Berlin using a high-tension cable, not carrying current, over the wall as his escape route. He inched his way along the cable while east German guards patrolled 60ft below.

**Sunday 3** — "£4.5 million Aid Schemes for the North" The Government provided further information about short- term construction work on roads, schools and hospitals for areas of high unemployment.

**Monday 4** — "Fords to Strike" About 1,500 TGWU members at the Ford plant at Dagenham agreed to a one-day official in protest at the company's refusal to reemploy 17 men it says are troublemakers.

## HERE IN BRITAIN

### "No Ballet for Fans"

Hundreds of balletgoers were turned away from the Royal Opera House, Covent Garden because of the danger of stucco falling from a cornice just below the roof. All doors except for the main entrance were closed which meant that the gallery and amphitheatre could not be used. The ballet programme, in which Dame Margot Fonteyn and Rudolf Nureyev danced together, continued as usual, but to an audience depleted by over a third. The performance had been booked up for several weeks and many had queued for hours to get their tickets. Despite this, the general attitude was one of resignation rather than anger.

## AROUND THE WORLD

### "Too Pricey Down Under"

About 300 South Africans who emigrated to Australia and New Zealand returned home, many saying they had come back because of the high cost of living. Some of the comments were: Houses to rent were 'almost unobtainable within a 20-mile radius of Sydney and very expensive'; food was 'fantastically priced'; 'many Australians have to take two jobs to make ends meet and there are any number of working wives' and 'it is a hard life for a woman, apart from housework, they run the vegetable gardens because of the prices of vegetables, especially in winter.'

# FIGHTING DISCRIMINATION

James Meredith, the pioneer of desegregation at the University of Mississippi, announced his decision to return for the spring term. He saw signs, he told a press conference in Jackson, Mississippi, which led him to hope that he would be able to study in the future under adequate, if not ideal, conditions.

In October of last year, a nine-hour battle was fought with tear gas, stones, bottles, and fire hoses, after it became known that federal marshals had brought a Negro applicant, on to the campus. The rioting continued throughout most of the night and early morning, but later that morning, Mr Meredith was officially enrolled in the administration building and walked to his first class amid angry, racist shouts but the slight 29-year-old student of political science made only one comment, *"This is not a happy occasion."*

Since then, he has lived day and night under the protection of federal marshals in a hostile atmosphere. It therefore came as no surprise when he expressed doubts recently about his ability to carry on, but he will obtain much sympathy and respect for his decision. Mr. Meredith said, *"For the past several days I have pondered this question. . . After listening to all arguments, evaluations and positions and weighing all this against my personal possibilities and circumstances, I have concluded that the 'Negro' should not return to the University of Mississippi. The prospects for him are too unpromising. However, I have decided that I, James Meredith, will register for the second semester of the University of Mississippi."* A number of those students who tried to befriend Mr. Meredith last term will not be returning because of the harassment they suffered. The chancellor of the university gave a warning that trouble-makers would not be tolerated.

# FEBRUARY 5TH - 11TH 1963

## IN THE NEWS

**Tuesday 5th**    **"They're Changing Pay at Buckingham Palace"** All the Queen's men have received a pay rise and improvements in their working conditions.

**Wednesday 6th**    **"New Blizzards Shut Roads to the West"** All roads from Exeter to London were blocked again and Cornwall was completely cut off. Over 100 people were stranded in two trains in Devon.

**Thursday 7th**    **"Great Thaw Starts – So Do the Floods"** A rapid thaw and torrential rain which will move over most of Britain, brought the peril of floods. As the 43-day grip of ice and snow was breaking, flood waters were pouring along roads in the south-west.

**Friday 8th**    **"Mr Wilson Tops Labour Leadership"** Beating his rival George Brown soundly in the first ballot, it looks as if Harold Wilson will be the new party leader and has a strong chance of going to No 10 as PM after the next General Election.

**Saturday 9th**    **"Coup d'Etat in Iraq"** General Kassim, who seized power in Iraq in a revolution in 1958, has himself been attacked and killed. The Iraq Air Force bombed or strafed the Premier's headquarters.

**Sunday 10th**    **"Cliff's Film Threatens Anglo-Yugoslav Friendship"** The Yugoslav Embassy regard as a 'scandalous insult', the scene in 'Summer Holiday' where four young mechanics who take a London bus through Europe are involved in a 'border incident' with Yugoslav customs officers.

**Monday 11th**    **"UK Nuclear Ship Plan"** Britain's first nuclear-powered merchant ship - possibly a 30,000-ton passenger liner-may be under construction next year and at sea by 1967.

### HERE IN BRITAIN
**"Fined if You Miss Your L-Test"**

Learner drivers who do not turn up for their tests are to be fined by forfeiting their £1 examination fee. Until now, this has been credited to them but because of the bad weather more than 332,000 people are waiting to take tests. Normally, 35,000 are tested every week. In the past few weeks, that number has dropped to 8,000. Unluckiest learners are those who applied for tests last November. They now go to the end of the queue – and may not get a test until May. Mr Marples has ordered the appointment of 100 more examiners to clear the backlog.

### AROUND THE WORLD
**"Fatal Importance of a Meat Pie"**

A Soviet district court has sentenced two men to be shot for saving fat on the frying of pirozhzkis (pies). The two men who organised the pie fraud were the director of the station restaurant at Sverdlovsk in the Urals, 850 miles east of Moscow, and the restaurant manager. The director invented an automatic fryer which saved two to three grams of fat on each pie compared with the amounts laid down in the regulations. This saving, however, was not passed on to customers in lower prices but 400 roubles a month (about £158) was shared out among the director and 55 accomplices.

# Fishermen In the Drink

**Grimsby trawlers being unloaded**

Owners of Hull's 140 trawlers are coming up to date with recruitment and training to overcome a traditional difficulty. They can no longer put the offender in the long boat until he sobers and have brought in an expert to help. *"It must be remembered that the modern trawler costs £30,000 or more and the equipment on its bridge is more highly technical than that of the Queen Elizabeth. As an industry we can no longer afford ridiculous accidents, either to the vessels or men."*

At present, men inquire for vacancies on the ships at the fish dock offices of the different firms at 9.30 every morning and deckhands, sometimes, because of the urgent need for crew, can slip by without completing seamanship courses.

In the meantime, when the trawler men return this month from three weeks or more at sea, they will receive a pamphlet spelling out the dangers of drunkenness. *"Although the days of the drunken, roughneck fisherman are long past"*, it reads, *"trouble is being caused by the small minority of men who think it is 'big' to get drunk before embarking on a trip."* Emphasizing that drinkers constituted only a handful of men, and most skippers do not mind men taking a bottle of Scotch or something with them - after they are going off to sea for 21 to 24 days after only three days at home – it says there are still too many cases of men trying to swim ashore from ships and drowning; falling over the side; ending up in hospital badly injured – or being killed.

However, the last word comes from a disenchanted deckhand, *"You try fishing around the North Cape in bad weather. You need to be a bit drunk or a bit daft even to consider going to work in those conditions."*

# FEBRUARY 12ᴛʜ - 18ᴛʜ 1963

## IN THE NEWS

**Tuesday 12**    **"Oyster Beds Wiped Out by Ice"** The severe weather will cause a shortage of oysters. The Kent and Essex coast produce more than half the eight million oysters eaten every year in Britain.

**Wednesday 13**    **"Queen Opens Parliament in New Zealand"** The Queen and the Duke of Edinburgh are now in New Zealand after their tours of Canada and Fiji. They will visit Australia next.

**Thursday 14**    **"Government Inquiry into Ford Strike"** The unions will call off the strike if the company resume making ex gratia payments of £11 per week to the 17 men dismissed as 'trouble-makers'.

**Friday 15**    **"My Recovery is Wonderful"** A Sheffield man in Leeds Infirmary is believed to be the first successful instance of a kidney being transplanted from a dead person to a living person.

**Saturday 16**    **"New Plot to Murder De Gaulle"** A woman teacher and four French Army men are under arrest after planning to shoot the President from a window when he inspected the Ecole Militaire in Paris.

**Sunday 17**    **"Ford Strike is Called Off"** In response to the Minister of Labour's appeal for normal work to continue while an official court of inquiry investigates the dispute of the 17 trouble-makers. They will be paid.

**Monday 18**    **"M1 Breakdowns"** Garages who attend breakdowns on the M1 will demand 'Cash on the Nail'. If they cannot pay, the car will be held at the garage until they can. The 13 garages who serve the M1 are owed thousands of pounds through bad debts.

---

### HERE IN BRITAIN

#### "Jet Age Spread"

The world's airlines are discovering the latest hazard of the new, fast, high-altitude jets. At 40,000 ft the falling air pressure is causing the glamorous air hostesses' clothes to become too tight. Some are finding the 'jet tummy' strain too much and slip off their tight girdles or even ask to be transferred to slower flights. Our bodies are built to withstand a certain air pressure, when this drops, the gases in the digestive system expand causing fullness and an embarrassing increase in girth. It seems to affect hostesses most and can take up to 24 hours for their waistlines to subside.

---

### AROUND THE WORLD

#### "Miss France Figures"

Muguette Fabris has found it is impossible to be the most beautiful girl in the world and continue teaching maths. Since being crowned Miss World last month, she has spent her weekends on tour, making guest appearances at casinos and music-halls but each Monday morning has been back at school. Now she has decided to give up teaching at her high school in Angouleme for a year to concentrate on the glamour. Her Headmistress is happy about this, *"I am fed up with this beauty business,"* she said, *"with all that makeup on her face this girl should not be teaching young children."*

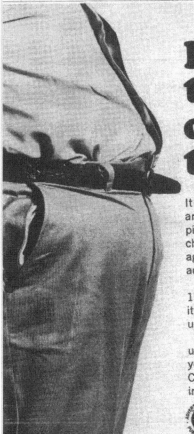

## Is this the shape of things to come?

It can be—with modern conveniences and push buttons. Easy living is sapping the strength and vitality of our children. One-third of them of school age can't pass minimum physical achievement tests.

Urge your school to offer at least 15 minutes of daily, vigorous activity. This can bring our nation's youth up to sound physical standards.

For a free booklet to help you evaluate the youth fitness program of your school, just write: President's Council on Physical Fitness, Washington 25, D.C.

President John F. Kennedy, an adherent of the active life who plays tennis and touch football, skies, swims, and skates whenever he can, is worried about the complacency with which many of his countrymen have come to view their health. Now he has discovered Roosevelt's 1908 order establishing the 50-mile march for officers and recently suggested that all United States troops should be tested for fitness by seeing whether they could walk 50 miles in 20 hours. This challenge has been taken up with an enthusiasm which almost surpasses belief in this country which hitherto has regarded walking as an intolerable inconvenience.

Many arrangements have been devised here to enable people to carry out their business without leaving their cars; you can eat in your car, cash cheques from your car, and spend an evening at the cinema without even opening the car door. Yet in the past weeks, soldiers and civilians alike, even pretty Washington secretaries, have taken to the roads on foot to see whether they can meet the President's requirements. In Pittsburgh more than 1,000 people set out to walk 28 miles to Washington, Pennsylvania. They did so with such vigour and apparent enjoyment that they were joined along the route by many more, so that at one time the harassed police estimated that there were more than 5,000 people walking along a four-lane highway.

At one point during the march, after the walkers had stopped for lunch at a restaurant, which afterwards estimated that it had served more than 1,200 sandwiches, 1,800 doughnuts, and 4,000 cups of coffee, a huge traffic jam developed and police urged the walkers to confine themselves to one lane. Many cars and a Red Cross unit followed the walkers to pick up any who fell out or to treat blisters. Those who reached Washington were returned to Pittsburgh in chartered buses.

# FEBRUARY 19TH - 25TH 1963

## IN THE NEWS

**Tuesday 19**  **"The Queen and Duke Arrive in Oz"** Greeted by a splendid reception and applause at Government House, the Queen within minutes had said, "This is not my last visit to Australia."

**Wednesday 20**  **"Khrushchev to Withdraw Russians from Cuba"** Russia informed the United States that the several thousand troops remaining in Cuba since last year will be withdrawn by March 15.

**Thursday 21**  **"Express Train Battle"** Seven masked bandits leaped from an express train near London after a fierce battle. The gang's target was 50 bags of mail in the brake van of the Euston-Holyhead Express, the Irish Mail.

**Friday 22**  **"£1.4m Bill for Skybolt"** This is part of the cost of the cancellation by America of the Skybolt missile which was to have provided the British independent nuclear deterrent.

**Saturday 23**  **"Russia Warns US of Cuba War Threat"** The Soviet Defence Minister warned the Americans that an attack on Cuba would mean a third world war in which the whole capitalist system would be *'buried once and for all'*. The US have asked for an explanation of a Soviet MiG fighter on a disabled American shrimp boat.

**Sunday 24**  **"Nessie Really Exists"** Millions of viewers saw the Loch Ness Monster splashing her way across the television screens. Nessie was filmed by searchlight in October, the 'experts' were led by Mr Peter Scott the naturalist.

**Monday 25**  **"Anglo-Us Jet Airliner Rivalry"** The de Havilland Trident made its maiden flight 13 months ahead of its American rival, the Boeing 727, but the American's have cut down the Trident delivery lead time.

## HERE IN BRITAIN

### "Electronic Parking"

An automatic ticket issuing system was introduced experimentally at a London Air Port car park. A car is halted at the entrance by a red and white painted barrier where a box containing the ticket equipment is on the driver's side and a bell rings when a vehicle passes over an electronic detector.

The driver takes the ticket from the machine, stamped with the date and time, and the barrier is automatically lowered when the car passes over a second detector. When a vehicle leaves it is halted by another barrier. The driver pays, and leaves when the attendant presses a button raising the barrier.

## AROUND THE WORLD

### "English 'As She is Spoken'"

English as spoken in some parts of England is not readily understood by Americans. This week a TV programme on the introduction of legal gambling in Britain used subtitles to translate a conversation between a Birmingham couple who were describing their reactions to winning the football pools.

The programme was conducted by Mr. David Brinkley, who speaks with a tight-lipped American drawl. No translation of his comments was provided, but he warned viewers before the Birmingham sequence that they might find it baffling.

# TOYS OF YESTERYEAR

This month a cache of Victorian toys, many of them in their original wrappings, was sold at auction and showed a stark contrast with the modern trend for toys to be more mechanical, scientific, sophisticated and expensive. The owner of the Victorian toys said that they were only brought out at the end of the day for a short time so that the children did not grow tired of them, nor were they broken. In this way the toys served two generations and lived to be seen and enjoyed 70 or 80 years later.

This year's International Toy Fair at Nuremberg attracted more than 1,000 exhibitors, showing 250,000 toys destined for the shops next Christmas. It is a serious business, *"you have got to have a gimmick if you're to sell a toy today",* a leading toy manufacturer declared a little sourly. For instance, some modern dolls from Japan play roulette, and some from France dance the Twist. Others cry so convincingly that a tender-hearted German reporter hurried over from an adjacent stand to see if he could pacify the 'child'.

The Americans have a Telstar communications satellite and there is also a Hovercraft from Britain, working on the lines of the real thing. The gimmick *can* work backwards though, a Noah's Ark displays the whole range of soft toy animals made by a west German firm and a pre-1914 model is used for a child's pedal car by a leading British one. There are 75 million children in Europe today and, for those adults who already think they have too many toys, the figure a head is still only a quarter of that in the United States. So long as Europe stays prosperous this is the big market that all manufacturers want to exploit.

# FEB 26ᵀᴴ - MARCH 4ᵀᴴ 1963

## IN THE NEWS

**Tuesday 26** "Tankers on Fire After Collision" Two women were among those rescued from the flame-covered water after a Panamanian tanker collided with a London tanker off Holland.

**Wednesday 27** "Pay Television Experiment" Organisations interested in the development of 'pay-as-you-view' are to take part in Britain's first experiment to show whether pay-television can find sufficient new programme material to justify itself.

**Thursday 28** "US Poaching Our Brains" Lord Hailsham, the Minister for Science, has claimed that *"America lives like a parasite on other people's brains."* His reason, the US education system has failed to produce their own.

**Friday March 1** "Coldest Winter for 133 Years" The Met Office figures show the average daily temperature at Kew for the past 3 months was 33.3 deg F (1degC), seven degrees colder than the normal 3 months average.

**Saturday 2** "Demand for Loans" London County Council received more than 3,000 inquiries from people interested in possible 100% mortgages of their valuation on houses and flats up to £5,000 and within 50 miles of Charing Cross.

**Sunday 3** "Rush on the Sunny Roads" Motorists bound for the seaside brought traffic generally to 40% above the average for the first Sunday in March. At the peak period 15,000 cars an hour were leaving London, mainly going to Brighton, Margate and Folkestone.

**Monday 4** "40-Hour Breakthrough" A big victory in the long campaign by unions for a 40-hour week in industry came in a three-year agreement on wages and benefits for contracting electricians who will receive pay rises *and* have their hours cut in autumn 1964.

## HERE IN BRITAIN
### "Rail Travel as Relaxation"

British Railways have a new slogan. *"Railway travel offers something more than mere transport - an interval of leisure, a retreat from the interruptions of modern life, freedom to relax and think."*
New first and second class carriages will have forced air heating and moulded fibreglass seats, station staff will have smart new uniforms and old stations will have new face lifts. Most striking are the new uniforms and in particular the caps. A continental flavour some might say, reminiscent of the Wehrmacht, the French Cavalry or the Grand Central!

## AROUND THE WORLD
### "Keeping Up With the Joneses"

Communist guards stationed at the Berlin wall had no sense of humour. 60 members of the London Welsh Choir split into two groups to travel to East Berlin where they had been invited to sing at a church. 30 went by coach via Checkpoint Charlie. 16 had the surname Jones and five were *John* Jones. The others went by train via the Friedrichstrasse checkpoint. 14 of them were called Evans and four were *John* Evans. The guards thought they were the victims of a big joke but were finally convinced – but they did have the last laugh, both parties were delayed for nearly two hours.

# FROZEN NEWTS ALIVE!

Moscow radio claimed in a broadcast to North America, that a creature resembling a lizard, found frozen into the ground at a depth of 25ft by Soviet geologists, came back to life for a time after being asleep for about 5,000 years. The creature, a vertebrate, had been classified as a four-toed triton, a primitive order of tailed amphibian. On awakening, they said, the lizard behaved exactly as it had done thousands of years ago. It ran around, ate and slept and was not afraid of people, eating wild berries, flies and mosquitoes from the hand. It died after three weeks, but another triton, found later at less depth, lived "practically all summer". The Soviets suggested that as these vertebrates could be brought back to life after so long a period, it might be possible to induce a similar state in human space travellers for their long trips to other planets. This would avoid the necessity for taking vast quantities of food and oxygen for the crew of a space craft.

The animal referred to as a triton is a newt and the article brought scepticism very quickly from an American expert who said it might be possible for tritons to have survived for 5,000 years, but he doubted it. Tests had indicated that salamanders, the modem form of tritons, could tolerate temperatures only a few degrees below freezing. Nor did it take long for an eminent *Soviet* scientist to describe the claim as 'pure invention'. The Professor remembered reading a children's book by a Siberian writer about two years ago who imagined geologists had found newts in the permanently frozen ground of the far North. The Professor had himself carried out experiments on a Siberian newt which had been frozen, and said, "If newts were frozen, they can never be revived."

# MARCH 5TH - 11TH 1963

## IN THE NEWS

**Tuesday 5**    **"Pentagon Pattern of Defence"** In an important constitutional change, the Government has decided to set up a unified Ministry of Defence. This will involve the abolition of the Admiralty, the War Office and the Air Ministry.

**Wednesday 6**    **"Waking Up to Warmth"** The 6th March was the first morning of the year without frost in Britain. Temperatures rose to 17 °C (62.6 °F) and the remaining snow disappeared.

**Thursday 7**    **"£100M Aircraft Order"** Shorts of Belfast are to get a big share of Hawker Siddeley Group's "plum" contract for a short take-off and landing tactical transport aircraft to replace the RAF's Hastings and Beverley piston-engine types.

**Friday 8**    **"Journalists Sent to Brixton"** Two Fleet Street journalists who refused to disclose their sources of information to the Vassall spy tribunal had their final petitions rejected and arrested to serve their sentences of six months' and three months' imprisonment.

**Saturday 9**    **"25 Guardsmen Go AWOL"** The men from the 1st Battalion, Scots Guards, were said to have met at a flat in Walworth, London yesterday morning to discuss complaints. *"They were discontented with all the bull."*

**Sunday 10**    **"Fanfare for Fords"** The first motor car to be assembled 'on Merseyside by Merseysiders' a lime green Anglia, was driven off the production line and through a triumphal arch at Ford's £30m Halewood factory yesterday by the Lord Mayor of Liverpool.

**Monday 11**    **"Bidault Seized by the Germans"** Georges Bidault, the hunted political leader of the anti-Gaullist OAS Secret Army, was seized by West German security police. He has requested asylum in Germany.

---

## HERE IN BRITAIN
### "The Cost of Z-Cars"

Drivers of Z-Cars, police squad cars – cost nearly £200 each to train but most motorists spend only £20 on lessons before taking a driving test. A squad car driver usually spends about 200 hours behind the wheel before qualifying and taking the current cost of driving lessons, this would work out to nearly £200 a driver.

A Ministry of Transport spokesman said that about one-third of L-drivers taking tests normally 'stood no chance of passing' and were 'wasting examiner's time' and that the Ministry was setting up a register which would act as a recognised qualification for driving instructors.

## AROUND THE WORLD
### "Weekend Cottage for Two"

During their tour of Australia, the Queen and the Duke of Edinburgh spent the weekend in a little white, weatherboard cottage, surrounded by kookaburras and wombats, on the beautiful upper reaches of the Snowy River.

Sunday, after attending the service in the tiny church, was a day of rest, which must have been welcome after the previous day when in eight hours, the Queen and the Duke drove 100 miles of the "Snowy Mountains Project", and "did", as the saying goes, two power stations, three dams and one tunnel, going underground twice in the process.

# PAN AM SKYSCRAPER

The Pan American building, a 59-storey skyscraper built over the railway lines of Grand Central Station in the heart of Manhattan, was officially opened this week. The building, the largest commercial office structure in the world, is owned jointly by the estate of the late Erwin S. Wolfson and by City Centre Properties Ltd of London. In a short speech, the President of the Board of Trade in New York, said it was fitting that the building should be the product of Anglo-American cooperation and that it would stand in the heart of New York as a visible reminder of the sometimes unobtrusive but always secure links between the two countries. The Pan Am building, named from its largest tenant, Pan American World Airways, who will occupy 15 floors, cost $100m. (£35,700,000).

Besides Pan American there will be about 100 other tenants and the chief reasons for the building's commercial success are its location, which could hardly be more convenient for commuters, and its modernity, which is perhaps most dramatically revealed in the creation of a helicopter station on its roof 808ft above the ground. The station is expected to be ready for operation in May and a frequent service to the three main New York airports will be inaugurated. It will then be possible to reach Idlewild in under 10 minutes (by any other means it takes three-quarters of an hour) and three 25-passenger turbo-jet helicopters can be accommodated on the half-acre landing pad at a time.

Apart from its commercial popularity, however, the building has come in for a good deal of criticism, chiefly because it will house another 20,000 people during working hours in an area which is already badly congested - a problem which has been greatly aggravated by the fact that about 50% of its office accommodation has been built in the past decade.

# MARCH 12TH - 18TH 1963

## IN THE NEWS

**Tuesday 12**  "Speeding Up Polaris" In order to minimize delay on the building of the first four British Polaris submarines only Vickers, Cammell Laird and Scotts, all with experience of submarine construction, can be considered.

**Wednesday 13**  "Minister to Impose Pay Scale" Sir Edward Boyle, the Minister of Education is to have his way on teachers' salaries giving him authority to redistribute the £21m in salary increases so that teachers with longer service, higher qualifications and greater responsibility will get more money.

**Thursday 14**  "Khrushchev Invited to Peking" The Soviet Union and China have agreed on the need to hold a summit meeting to thrash out their ideological differences.

**Friday 15**  "Mystery of the Missing Model" Christine Keeler who was to have been a key witness against John Edgecombe, the man accused of trying to murder her, has vanished.

**Saturday 16**  "Paris Rebuff to Foreign Secretary" Another slap at the already strained Anglo-French relations – M. Couve de Murville, the French Foreign Minister, has publicly snubbed Lord Home by turning down an invitation to lunch.

**Sunday 17**  "Guards to Stand Less on Ceremony" Moves to make life brighter for the Scots Guards and boost morale are a guarantee of time off after duty at Windsor Castle. 25 Guards staged a protest earlier this month.

**Monday 18**  "Now Its Ten Cases of Typhoid" Another two cases were confirmed in Cardiff and like the other eight cases in southern England, they had all returned from winter sports in Zermatt, Switzerland where there are 55 suspected cases.

---

## HERE IN BRITAIN
### "Murder on Parole"

Two hours after he committed murder, George Thatcher rang the bell at Pentonville jail and was let in by a prison officer. He was one of the men chosen to take part in the hostel scheme, designed to prepare long-term prisoners for their return to society which meant he was able to work outside in an ordinary job by day and return to prison at night.

It meant too, that he could take part in the Mitcham Co-op robbery last November and shoot dead a lorry driver. He was sentenced to death at the Old Bailey and three accomplices, sentenced to life imprisonment.

## AROUND THE WORLD
### "Stone Age Natives"

A tribe of 100, curious and helpful natives have been found in Papua New Guinea. They were stumbled upon by an administration patrol in a hamlet on a hilltop in the Sepik district and they invited the patrolmen to their main village of G'hom. The G'homs live a semi-nomadic existence, spending most of their time hunting, fishing and gathering food and had never travelled beyond their linguistic area. The men wear kilts of woven bark cloth, the women knee length grass skirts and all had their noses pierced with flying fox bones. They make their own clay crockery and cook opossums, waterfowl, sago, and yams.

# ESTATE CARS RULE

Humber Super Snipe

Morris 1000 Traveller

Ford Anglia Estate

Mini Traveller

Buyers saw the latest British estate cars on show at the Geneva Motor Show. Today, these multi-purpose motor cars amount for 12% of sales in Britain and are bought by one in 10 of overseas motorists. Detroit inspired the trend towards 'hunting, shooting, fishing', family-carrying station wagons, but their popularity and style have swept far beyond the old conception of riverside barbecues and varnished woodwork. The estate car has evolved into a spacious, swift, sophisticated saloon, with all the performance of its conventional counterpart, but as suitable for dining at the Ritz as for loading up with logs or dogs.

Ford's managing director attributes the estate car boom to the growing family desire for more living space in family cars. *"Many thousands of us go for our annual holiday on the Continent and expect to be able to drive to the south of France and back, complete with family, in comfort and certainty."* In addition, mounting city congestion and a general trend towards out-of-town dwelling has helped.

The choice in estate cars is now as wide as in any other type, and prices range from £500 to more than £2,000, though the most popular models are in the 1-litre £700-£1,200 class. Woodwork is still with us on a few models but is about to be ousted by an extremely tough vinyl sheeting known as Di-Noc and the all-steel station wagon is easier to keep clean.

At the top of the British 6-seater range are the £1,565 Humber Super Snipe, the middle range has the comfortable 1.6 litre Hillman Super Minx at £804. The Austin A40 Countryman and Morris Minor Traveller at £576 and £582 compete with the Ford Anglia estate at £575 and in Mini size, there is a choice of Austin or Morris Mini Traveller for £532 – each with surprising capacity.

# MARCH 19TH - 25TH 1963

## IN THE NEWS

**Tuesday 19**    **"New Cases of Typhoid"** This brings the total number in Britain to 24, the first ten all connected to winter sports trips to Zermatt in Switzerland.

**Wednesday 20** **"Higher Post Office Prices"** Telegrams, parcels and trunk telephone calls will all go up in a bid to bring in £14m. net extra in a full year.

**Thursday 21**    **"First Driverless Train"** The first automatic trains on the London underground, now on trials, could be in operation within three weeks, the government has revealed.

**Friday 22**    **"Minister and Model: Deny or Investigate"** A sensational challenge was flung down in the Commons when a Labour MP asked Mr Macmillan to investigate rumours involving a 'member of the Government Front Bench' and Miss Christine Keeler, Miss Marilyn Davies and a shooting by a West Indian.

**Saturday 23**    **"Mr Profumo Ignorant of Witness's Whereabouts"** In an unusually filled Commons, the Minister of War explained that he had not seen Miss Keeler since 1961 and that there was no impropriety between them.

**Sunday 24**    **"Cut Foreign Aid"** President Kennedy was advised to reduce the amount and scope of foreign aid and persuade others to take up more of the burden. Britain was included in a list of countries that should be asked to do more, and only France was absolved from the sins of hard loans and tied exports.

**Monday 25**    **"Miss Keeler Found"** The missing trial witness whose disappearance caused a storm, is in Madrid apparently blissfully unaware of the furore surrounding her whereabouts.

## HERE IN BRITAIN

### "Refused a Lick and a Promise"

When an assistant in Barnsley post office, Yorkshire, pushed postage stamps, gummed side down, across the counter, Mr Elmhirst refused to lick them.

The customer, a farmer and local councillor said, *"It is about time a machine, similar to those used at cinemas for issuing tickets, was used. It would be far more hygienic. We have to breathe the foul air of Barnsley but there is no reason why we should eat the dirt off the counter. On this occasion I insisted on a pad being found to wet the stamps. The next time I shall get in touch with the Postmaster General."*

## AROUND THE WORLD

### "Top Hats and Fur Caps"

The Maharaj Kumar of Sikkim took Hope Cooke of New York as his Princess this week. They married on a flat-topped hill, its sides falling steeply away into valley depths and behind, the distant peaks of Kanchenjunga.
Several thousand locals watched the guests arrive, top hats and striped trousers mingling with fur-flapped caps and high boots of mountain men.
Saris, gleaming gems and bold gold finery of the Nepali womenfolk vied with many of the ladies who had come from New York and London, who wore the same kind of hat, a clutch of petals - much to the amusement of the locals.

# WHO'S FAIR FOR FAIR ISLE?

Fair Isle

Scotland

BOOK OF FAIR ISLE KNITTING

Birds might outnumber people on Fair Isle by hundreds to one, but some of the people are rare birds too. The National Trust for Scotland, owners of Fair Isle, require unusual qualities in tenants who are offered crofts there. Apart from the ability to handle a boat, experience of clipping sheep and knowledge of wildlife are regarded as advantages for male applicants. A wife who knits also raises the points in an applicant's favour.

The island was acquired by the trust in 1954, has a population of just over 40 who make a living from sheep, crofting, lobster fishing and handcrafts, including knitting, especially the traditional island patterns, and weaving. A century ago, the population numbered 300 but 30 years ago this had dropped to 100. The Trust are maintaining the level of the population by attracting adventurous people who are not only physically fit but adaptable to the markedly communal way of life. A certain amount of capital is required by the new tenants, but they cannot buy their way into a croft, they are selected by a system which correlates their aptitude to the amount of capital they are prepared to invest.

Applicants must answer 23 questions, stating whether they have any interest or knowledge of birds or other wildlife; experience of living on an island during the winter months; if they are prepared to live in a rough climate with frequent winter gales; and other points including why they want to settle on Fair Isle. Some lose interest when they see what the questionnaire suggests is in store for them and an English woman who made corsets and who was inquiring about a croft for herself and her husband, was not, on the strength of superficial details, considered to be a wholly useful recruit for the community!

# MARCH 26TH - APRIL 1ST 1963

## IN THE NEWS

**Tuesday 26**    **"Doctors and Dentists to Get 14% More"** There are more than 24,000 hospital doctors and dentists in Britain, and nearly 23,000 doctors and 12,000 dentists in general practice. The average net income of a GP will rise to £2,765 and dentists, to £2,740.

**Wednesday 27**    **"5,000 Besiege Parliament"** 500 police, mounted and on foot, were involved in serious clashes outside Parliament yesterday during a lobby of MPs by Trades Union members representing the unemployed.

**Thursday 28**    **"Railways to be Slashed"** Large parts of the British railway system are uneconomic and under-used, a report by Dr Richard Beeching has declared. Only half the network's routes carry enough traffic to cover the cost of operating them.

**Friday 29**    **"Outcry in Zermatt"** Whilst hotels and restaurants have now shut and tourists deserted the Swiss winter sports resort, there is an outcry that the authorities have been trying to keep the outbreak of typhoid quiet so as not to scare off wealthy tourists.

**Saturday 30**    **"Kennedy Faces New Cuba Crisis"** There have been attacks by Cuban exiles based in America on Russian ships and two MiG fighters from Havana fired across the bows of an American cargo ship.

**Sunday 31**    **"African Break Up"** Sir Roy Welensky, Premier of the Central African Federation, raged at the Government after their agreement to Northern Rhodesia withdrawing and thereby ending the ten year Federation.

**Monday 1 Apr**    **"Odds On Rail Strike"** The National Union of Railwaymen have called Dr Beeching's plan "suicide" and called for national strike action.

## HERE IN BRITAIN
### "Too Much Money at the Mint"

Officials at the Royal mint have found that for 20 years they have overpaid their staff. One hundred night-shift workers from the staff of 800 at the 'money factory' near the Tower of London, have been receiving overtime rates of between 10s and £1 a week, and now it has been discovered that they were never entitled to it.

The mistake arose from a misunderstanding with the TGWU and now the men have been warned that deductions may be necessary. A Mint employee said, *"It seems rather an embarrassing situation for the place that produces the country's small change."*

## AROUND THE WORLD
### "A Play Not to be Sneezed At"

Actors jumped from the stage to exchange blows with hissing and booing playgoers at a performance in Paris of M. Jean Cau's controversial play 'Les Parachutistes'. The play is set in Algeria and refers to torture by French troops and atrocities by Algerian nationalists. Throughout the first act a noisy group of students demonstrated and whistled and then a cloud of sneezing powder caused the whole audience at the theatre, on the Champs Elysees, to cough and sneeze. Interruptions continued and fighting broke out after the interval but the actors finally returned to the stage shouting, *"Let us carry on with the job."*

# STAFF FOR HIRE

As the guests filed slowly past the bride and groom, the footmen stood, erect as guardsmen, resplendent in pale blue livery, serving glasses of champagne, but weddings, stately house parties and embassies are not the only occasions for which one can hire staff. At other times, footmen will serve at dinners and cocktail parties where they resent any confusion with waiters who, they point out, have not been trained in private service. Demand for footmen at 35s (£1.75) an evening, and butlers at 21 guineas (£22), reaches a peak during the season. For a house party, when duties are more onerous and hours much longer, a butler costs three guineas a day and a footman 45s (£2.25) plus the cost of their keep.

Only a few establishments now employ a big staff - comprising butler, cook, footman, two housemaids, kitchen maid, lady's maid, chauffeur-handyman and dailies, at a cost of about £6,000 a year. This would cover pay, food, heating and lighting and uniforms.

Still at the pinnacle of domestic service stands the butler, many of whom "have all the benefits of a £2,000 a year man". To their pay and keep must be added tips, a new suit each year and the use of the family's second car on days off. Today there are probably no more than 600 butlers, but his influence still remains.

One butler told of a couple who arrived at a weekend house party with nine suitcases. The lady's maid was for ever running up and down three flights of stairs on errands ranging from fetching newspapers to refilling the hot-water bottle for breakfast in bed. On their departure, the car boot had to be unpacked and a suitcase opened to find a suitable shade of headscarf for the journey back. "The news", said the butler, "reached the master. It is unlikely that they will be invited again."

# APRIL 2ND - 8TH 1963

## IN THE NEWS

**Tuesday 2**    **"17 Held in Bahamas"** The Government, in collaboration with the US, has acted on the dangerous situation in the Caribbean. Police landed by air on an island in the Bahamas and detained 17 men whom the frigate, HMS Londonderry, took on to Nassau.

**Wednesday 3**    **"Moon Station Launched"** Russia launched her fourth unmanned moon rocket, Lunik IV, to pioneer the way for a landing by man. The probe carries the "Automatic Moon- IV" station and is expected to reach the vicinity of the moon in three and a half days.

**Thursday 4**    **"Maudling's Brew"** Chancellor Reginald Maudling released £270m spending money to the taxpayers in his budget planning for a boost in national prosperity – and scrapped the licence duty on home-made-beer!

**Friday 5**    **"Govt. Will Check New Drugs"** In the wake of the thalidomide scandal, a 'watchdog' committee is to guard the public against unnecessary danger from new drugs.

**Saturday 6**    **"US – Soviet Telephone Link"** Mr Kennedy and Mr Khrushchev are to have a "hot line" which should reduce the risk of nuclear war being caused by accident or misunderstanding.

**Sunday 7**    **"Soviet Silence on 'Lunik IV'"** The Russian moon rocket returned towards earth after passing 5,300 miles from the moon. The automatic station will orbit the earth and eventually become a satellite of the sun.

**Monday 8**    **"Thaw on the Western Front"** Lord Home, the Foreign Secretary, is in Paris for a meeting of the South East-Asia Treaty Organisation. His visit gives the French authorities a chance to repair relations since the breakdown of the Common Market negotiations.

## HERE IN BRITAIN
### "The Village Number Puzzle"

So many visitors got lost in Cranborne, Dorset that the council ordered villagers to number their houses. Unfortunately, there were no name plates on any of the 12 streets and now things are worse than before. The streets do have names but only the villagers know them – and even they are not always sure! One woman who for 30 years thought she lived in Swan Street now finds that her address is The Alley. The village draper has refused until the council put up name plates and risks a £2 fine. *"It is ridiculous to put the cart before the horse like this."*

## AROUND THE WORLD
### "They Meant it Most Sincerely"

A Russian MiG fighter fired warning shots around Hughie Green's plane as he piloted it over East Germany. He was flying his Cessna from Stuttgart to Berlin and was over one of the recognised air corridors linking West Germany with Berlin when the MiGs suddenly appeared out of heavy cloud, one on each side, and began wagging their wings telling him to land. When he refused, one of the fighters fired several shots near his plane. Mr Green, perfectly within the rules, maintained his course and landed safely at the RAF airfield in Berlin and the protests to Russia began.

# THE POOR LITTLE TWEENY

The days of the *'poor little tweeny'* are gone, according to a booklet circulated in the high unemployment areas of the north. 'Service in the Sixties', prepared by a London employment agency, represents the latest attempt to attract young women into domestic service. Before the war the tweeny - a maid with duties divided between house and kitchen - symbolized to many the overworked, underpaid woman servant. But now, the booklet says, *'household employment has developed, matured, grown up'*. A state of unpleasant servitude has given way to a career that provides opportunities for travel and *'the fascination of seeing in real life the people you have read about in the newspapers and seen on television'*.

However, attempts to attract women into domestic work since the war have mostly proved unsuccessful. Since 1945 the numbers employed privately have about halved and the figure now stands at just over 220,000 with many daily 'helps' swelling even this reduced number. As a result, it is becoming increasingly difficult and often impossible to meet the demand for staff. Mothers' helps and general maids are extremely lacking, good cooks are scarce and at the same time the need for daily 'helps' at between 5s and 7s an hour, has never been so great. Also much in demand is the traditional nanny. *'We can never get enough of them'*, the director of a London employment agency said, "there are now families, mostly in the £2,500 to £5,000 income range, looking for nannies who would not have employed them before the war.

What is it then that makes domestic work so unattractive to women in Britain? One view is that many still think of the occupation as it was before the war. Another is that there is a *'social stigma'* to domestic employment, and that *'girls are ashamed to tell their boyfriends that they are maids'*.

# APRIL 9TH - 15TH 1963

## IN THE NEWS

**Tuesday 9**    **"Factories for Development Areas"** The Government is to sponsor 13 more factories in the north, Scotland and Wales, plus 15 more retraining centres, and the Minister appealed to industry and to the unions to go ahead with shorter apprenticeships.

**Wednesday 10**    **"Petrol Wars Hot Up"** As an Italian firm, AGIP, opened their first filling station here, one of America's Continental Oil – who already own Jet, who sell petrol at 3d (1p) a gallon cheaper – announced plans for a new chain called Conoco UK.

**Thursday 11**    **"US Nuclear Sub Missing"** The US Navy announced that the nuclear submarine Thresher, with 129 men on board, was 'overdue and presumed missing' in the Atlantic.

**Friday 12**    **"Blizzards Mar Holiday"** Blizzards in the north, snow showers in Devon and Cornwall and sunshine and traffic jams in the south marked the start of the Easter holiday. Snowfalls up to 8in were reported in parts of Scotland.

**Saturday 13**    **"Anti-Nuclear Booklet Discloses Secrets"** Secret details of the system of government in the event of a nuclear attack on Britain were leaked and published by 'Spies for Peace'.

**Sunday 14**    **"Railways to be Slashed by a Quarter"** The rail unions have given the Government one month to soften the impact of Dr Beeching's plan announced last month, or they will call a national rail strike.

**Monday 15**    **"Loss of US Submarine"** The Queen sent a message of condolence to President Kennedy on the confirmation of the loss of the US submarine 'Thresher'. All men on board who included civilian technicians have perished.

## HERE IN BRITAIN

### "A Small Penny Farthing"

Arthur, a bicycle maker aged 73 is about to have his life-long wish come true. At 5ft 3in he has always been too short to ride a penny-farthing but his firm, Falcon in Smethwick, has said he can now make one to fit. This is because Arthur was brought out of retirement to make a penny-farthing to display on the company stand at a cycle show.

An American buyer spotted it and liked it so much he ordered 100 at £100 each. Now he wants a smaller version made which Arthur should be able to ride or if not, he can 'tailor-make' one.

## AROUND THE WORLD

### "Golden Easter Surprise"

On Easter morning Russian royalty had a very special kind of celebration. Towards the latter part of the nineteenth century Carl Faberge, a Russian-born goldsmith of Huguenot extraction, was given permission by the Tsar Alexander III to make a surprise egg for the Tsarina. For Easter 1895, he made an egg of gold, enamelled white, inside which was a golden yolk and inside that again sat a gold and white hen with ruby eyes. This was presented to the Tsarina and gave such pleasure that surprise eggs became an annual event. Moreover, the craftsmanship was so superb that Faberge became world-famous.

# CHURCHILL BECOMES A US CITIZEN

The President of the United States of America

A PROCLAMATION

Whereas

## Sir Winston Churchill

*a son of America though a subject of Britain, has been throughout his life a firm and steadfast friend of the American people and the American nation; and*

*Whereas he has freely offered his hand and his faith in days of adversity as well as triumph; and*

*Whereas his bravery, charity and valor, both in war and in peace, have been a flame of inspiration in freedom's darkest hour; and*

*Whereas his life has shown that no adversary can overcome, and no fear can deter, free men in the defense of their freedom; and*

*Whereas he has expressed with unsurpassed power and splendor the aspirations of peoples everywhere for dignity and freedom; and*

President Kennedy presents the proclamation to Churchill's son Randolph . Sir Winston was too ill to attend.

Sir Winston Churchill was this month declared by proclamation an honorary citizen of the United States, in a ceremony at the White House. Citizen Churchill, in a letter, said that it was an honour without parallel *'which he accepted with deep gratitude and affection'*. The proclamation was read by Mr Kennedy from the steps that lead from his office to the rose garden, in the presence of Mrs. Kennedy, Mr Randolph Churchill, and his son, Winston. Mr Randolph Churchill, who read his father's letter, received the passport specially prepared for Sir Winston, the only document of its kind. The form of the ceremony was dictated by the requirements of transatlantic television and was scheduled such that this unique honour could be watched live by millions of viewers, in Britain as well at the US.

President Kennedy declared, *"We mean to honour him, but his acceptance honours us far more. No proclamation can enrich his name, the name Sir Winston Churchill is already a legend. He is the most honoured and honourable man to walk the stage of human history in the time in which we live. Whenever and wherever tyranny threatens, he has always championed liberty."*

Sir Winston now aged 88, who stirred even neutralist Americans in 1940 with his call for blood, tears, toil and sweat, watched the ceremony with Lady Churchill on television at his London home. He sat smoking a cigar whilst his son expressed the *"deep gratitude and affection"* of his father at the ceremony. The hope was that Sir Winston would respond on the satellite relay, but this was not to be. Apart from any possible indisposition on his part, the relay station at Goonhilly, Cornwall, was not ready to transmit and somebody decided against asking the French help on this very special Anglo-American occasion!

53

# APRIL 16ᵀᴴ - 22ᴺᴰ 1963

## IN THE NEWS

**Tuesday 16**    **"Ban the Bomb Clashes"** 70 people were arrested in London yesterday when many thousands of 'Ban-the-bomb' marchers from Aldermaston fought with police on their route through the West End to a mass rally in Hyde Park.

**Wednesday 17**    **"Home Office Gave Me Secrets"** A former member of the anti-nuclear Committee of 100 denied being responsible for the "Spies for Peace" pamphlet circulated on the eve of the Aldermaston march but said about 40% cent of the information had been divulged to him months ago.

**Thursday 18**    **"Wynne Charged as Soviet Spy"** Greville Wynne, the British businessman is to provide one of Russia's biggest most spectacular spy trials when he is brought before a military court in Moscow.

**Friday 19**    **"Flexible Skirts to Make Smoother Ride"** Long 'skirts' will allow Hovercraft to travel better over rough surfaces and the Isle of Wight based, Westland Aircraft, is to produce a new model, the SRN5.

**Saturday 20**    **"Gas Affects 20 After Tanker Crash"** Twenty people, including a two-day- old baby, were taken to hospital when ammonia gas escaped and spread over a wide area, from a tanker jammed under Atlas Road bridge, Darwen, Lancashire.

**Sunday 21**    **"Camouflage on the Roads"** Post Office green, used by the GPO for their vehicles and equipment, is quoted, in The Ophthalmic Optician, as an example of dangerous camouflage that motorists encounter every day.

**Monday 22**    **"Fishermen Request a 12-mile Limit"** In light of the Danish and Icelandic decisions on a 12-mile fishing limit, British inshore fishermen want our 3 mile limit extended.

## HERE IN BRITAIN
### "No Need to be Plain Jane"

Everyone knew that the hairdresser was a girl's best friend, said the President of the National Hairdressers' Federation. In the past 21 years the craft of hairdressing has radically altered. The number of salons has increased from 30,000 to 40,000 and great technical changes have been made, but it was probably in hair colour that most advances have occurred.

Nearly one woman in five now uses colour, *"whereas then it was restricted to those few who were prepared to defy convention and were in danger of being stigmatised as 'brazen', 'brassy', or frankly immoral, especially if their hair was bleached".*

## AROUND THE WORLD
### "Golden Coins"

The Treasury in Nuku'alofa, capital of the kingdom of Tonga, put in circulation the first coins ever produced by the Friendly Islands. Minted in gold at the Royal Mint in London, the coins are the first gold coins to be issued within the area of Polynesia.

They are also the first gold coins to be placed in unrestricted circulation at face value as part of a national currency since the devaluation of world gold more than 30 years ago. This is also the first time for over 150 years that the Royal Mint has produced a coinage in gold alloyed only with silver.

# GARBAGE TO GOLD

*Mary-Soo's women cleaning a warship. They cleaned the outside and all of the crew quarters.*

Mary-Soo is a sun-burnt, weather-beaten Cantonese who has never worn a cheongsam in all her 50 years, but she has enterprise, and she is a wealthy woman. Out of the turmoil of the Second World War she has built a flourishing business cleaning out the ships of the US Navy. Fifteen years ago, Mary-Soo wriggled her sampan alongside one of the American warships lying in Hong Kong harbour to take on garbage. She tossed her slippers on the deck, climbed carefully aboard, and stood watching the sailors scrubbing, painting and polishing. She decided she could do the work better herself. Mary-Soo offered her services to the US naval authorities. She would supply a team of women, brushes, paint and rollers and clean inside and outside all US naval ships in the harbour, collect all garbage and dispose of it. The sailors could go ashore and enjoy themselves. Her offer was accepted.

Garbage is Mary-Soo's special interest, for good money is paid for garbage in overcrowded Hong Kong. Her dealers are lined-up and ready on the quayside. Edible 'left-overs' go to the farmers for pig-food, surplus stocks of meat and vegetables are sold 'at a higher price of course' - to the Chinese restaurants. Old blankets, boxes, crates, scrap-iron and so on have a ready market. The scrap-iron is turned into pots and pans. Mary-Soo will not employ men. Girls are easier to handle and make no trouble. *"They are always happy"*, she will explain, *"and in Hong Kong women work harder than men"*. The US Navy is well content with the arrangement. When the cleaning-out is finished the ships are decorated with fresh flowers, from the captain's room to the men's quarters, and as the fleet leaves port Mary-Soo and her fleet of sampans wobble alongside firing a farewell salute with strings of Chinese firecrackers.

# APRIL 23RD - 29TH 1963

## IN THE NEWS

**Tuesday 23**    **"Navy Polaris Base for Scotland"** The British Polaris submarines will operate from a base at Faslane in the Gare Loch.

**Wednesday 24**    **"Princess Alexandra of Kent Marries"** Thousands of well-wishers lined the streets and millions watched on television as the Queen's cousin married The Hon. Angus Ogilvy.

**Thursday 25**    **"Anglo-US Approach to Khrushchev"** Mr Macmillan and President Kennedy sent a joint letter to the Soviet leader in a new attempt to break the deadlock and raising hopes of finalising a treaty to ban nuclear tests.

**Friday 26**    **"New North Sea Oil Ventures"** A consortium of British shipyards have joined forces with major oil companies in a full-scale search for natural gas (and possibly oil) under the bed of the North Sea.

**Saturday 27**    **"Delay for the Divorce Bill"** Mr. Leo Abse's controversial Bill making seven years' separation a ground for divorce will be delayed by the debate that will take place on amendments to a different Bill, thus going to the bottom of the list and not heard.

**Sunday 28** "    **Castro Given a Hero's Welcome in Moscow"** Mr. Khrushchev embraced and hugged Fidel Castro, the Cuban Prime Minister, hailed him as a 'popular hero' and 'envoy of the first socialist country on the American continent', and pledged continued Soviet support for the Cuban revolution.

**Monday 29**    **"Gunboat Chases Trawler"** An Aberdeen trawler was chased by an Icelandic coastguard gunboat which fired blank shots. The Navy's fishery protection frigate, HMS Palliser, was sent to investigate.

## HERE IN BRITAIN

### "Chicken Quarrels Mean Less Eggs"

Chickens can spend their whole life being henpecked. Experts claim that the trouble starts when hens are allowed to mix freely, *"Within any flock there is a social structure, a hierarchy of superior birds to be avoided by inferior birds. Only the boss bird can walk anywhere.*

*However, a hen can only recognise about 30 of her companions hence small back garden flocks lay better than large flocks.*

*Here each bird knows to avoid its superior but if she must move outside her own circle to get food, water or nest boxes, then fights happen, the flock becomes nervous and egg production goes down."*

## AROUND THE WORLD

### "A Black Panther Goes to School"

A black panther escaped from a circus in northern Paris and was recaptured alive, dripping and furious after a defiant and tense six-hour siege underneath a girls' elementary school.

The pupils had been evacuated when an alert teacher realised, and cages and nets were set up, holes were drilled through the school's concrete foundations and floors, and tear gas bombs thrown in followed by jets of water from a high-pressure hose.

All this only made the panther, angrier and when finally, two circus tamers drove it to the trap, the cage trembled as the panther leaped-in, snarling furiously at the cheering crowd.

# SPY REPORT WHITEWASH

*Moscow Kremiln, Red Square and St Basil Cathedral*

Last October, another spy went to prison. In court, the Attorney General said, "You have been well rewarded, and you have sold some part of the safety and security of the people of this country for cash". William Vassall, a £14-a-week clerk in the Admiralty was sentenced to 18 years for offences under the Official Secrets Act. The Lord Chief Justice told him, "One of the compelling reasons for what you did was pure selfish greed. You have said in your statement to the police that you had no intention of harming this country. I am quite unable to accept that. A man of your education, intelligence and experience knew full well that this information and these documents would be directly of assistance to an enemy."

Since October, a committee of inquiry has been investigating and their report published this week, has taken 50,000 words to find that *"no one is held to blame for Vassall's not being detected earlier."* Even though senior officers at the Embassy in Moscow did not follow up warnings from an Embassy typist, Mary Wynne, who realised a junior interpreter employed at the Embassy was in fact a fully-fledged Russian agent, who being a homosexual too, targeted Vassall and led him into the spy trap.

It is now apparent that Vassall was a security risk on three main counts. He had served behind the Iron Curtain as a bachelor, he is a homosexual and he lived, quite obviously, beyond his salary. While those responsible could hardly be expected to know all the details of his private life, it is not too much to expect that some suspicion should have been aroused. Had even the previous vetting procedures, now considerably tightened, been rigorously applied in his case, suspicion should have been aroused at least three years before when he moved into a flat in prestigious Dolphin Square.

# APRIL 30TH - MAY 6TH 1963

## IN THE NEWS

**Tuesday 30**    **"Mr K Buys British"** The president of the Russian machinery purchasing organization called Techmashimport, has placed two orders worth a total of £26m to bring Russia's plastics industry up to western standards.

**Wed 1 May**    **"Marples on the Rack"** Tory MPs rebelled and abstained from voting with the government after the transport minister was 'massacred' in the debate on the Beeching Report.

**Thursday 2**    **"Sir Winston Churchill to Resign"** Parliament's greatest figure of the century is to stand down as an MP at the next General Election after more than 60 of the last 63 years in the Commons.

**Friday 3**    **"Stars and Stripes on Everest"** Ten years after the British first conquered Mount Everest, the first American attempt has succeeded and two men have reached the summit.

**Saturday 4 "**    **Hillman Imp Released"** The four-seater, four-cylinder Hillman Imp is the first mass-produced British car to have a rear-mounted aluminium engine and the first car to be made in Scotland for more than 30 years.

**Sunday 5 "**    **Alabama at Flash Point"** Racial tension came close to flash point in Birmingham, Alabama. More than 1,600 demonstrators have been taken into custody in a month having been faced with high-pressure water hoses and police dogs.

**Monday 6**    **"Warship Stands by to Evacuate British"** Refugees from Haiti told of the 'blood bath' ordered by President Duvalier. 186 Army officers and anti-Government supporters had been *'shot like dogs'* by the Ton Ton Macautes – Duvalier's army of Negro thugs.

### HERE IN BRITAIN

#### "Song and Dance at Tomato Board"

Continuing to ridicule the Tomato and Cucumber Marketing Board, Larry White, a Yorkshire grower, turned up at the annual meeting as a minstrel in pink and white trousers, bow tie and boater. To the strains of "Swanee River" he tap-danced his way up the marble stairway of Agriculture House, Knightsbridge, followed by banjo and accordion.

Mr. Wright, who is chairman of the board's publicity committee, claimed with some justification, that he attracted more free publicity for tomatoes and cucumbers than anybody else.

### AROUND THE WORLD

#### "Every American Will Have a Number"

Everyone in the United States is to be given a five-figure number to attach to their name and address. The use of the numbers on envelopes will speed postal deliveries and will be called the zip number. They will assist the mechanical handling of letters and tell sorting machines the area, state, city and postal zone in which the addressee lives.

Ultimately this number will have to be used on all United States mails, but it is not envisaged that its use will do away with the need for a name and address, though the addition of four more digits could make even this possible.

# BRINGING MUSEUMS ALIVE

*The Elgin Marbles (main Photo) and modern interactive displays in The Science Museum.*

A fresh and constructive approach to the display of objects in museums and public galleries, is exemplified in the redesigned presentation of the Science Museum's collections of sailing ships and small craft. The old image of a museum - a miscellany of objects, meagerly labelled and huddled in somewhat unprepossessing, dusty cases - is being updated with the purpose of better engaging the attention of the public by more imaginative and informative presentation.

Logical arrangement and placing of the objects; background colour, texture and lighting and the use of photographs, drawings or dioramas accompanied by clearly legible lettering and printed descriptions. The effect of a work of art can be entirely spoilt by an unsuitable background or juxtaposition and attention is now given to these factors with the use of variously coloured fabrics and materials sympathetic in character with the exhibits. It has been realised that colour has a psychological importance for the spectator; a change of scheme from one display to another prevents visual fatigue and creates a repeated renewal of interest.

However, the methods being introduced have met with some objections. There are scholars who fear it is destroying the atmosphere of scholarship by popularisation. Some deplore the idea of 'dolling up' a museum but this *can* be the rational solution to two big problems. An ordered arrangement brought about by 'primary' collections and separate study collections according to subject and using to best advantage, the huge buildings designed without regard for the scale and display of the objects they were to contain. Ideally, a museum should be planned from the start for its type of content as in the Elgin Marbles room at the British Museum, specially constructed to house the Parthenon sculptures, which, if architecturally retaining its past grandiosity, showcases the Greek masterpieces to much better advantage than before.

## IN THE NEWS

**Tuesday 7**  **"NUR to Call Tube Drivers Out"** However, they are prepared to meet Dr Beeching for talks as '*long as we get something*' and in particular, a plan to ease redundancies.

**Wednesday 8**  **"Commission Proposed for Spy Cases"** In the wake of the recent Vassall case and Inquiry, Mr Macmillan invited the Commons to consider whether a permanent security commission should be set up to investigate the background of cases of espionage.

**Thursday 9**  **"Duke of Argyll Granted a Divorce"** At the end of a notorious and marathon divorce case against his glamorous wife, the Duke declared, "*What a relief, it's high time but it will cost me a hell of a lot of money.*"

**Friday 10**  **"Railmen Call Off Their Strike"** The three-day strike threatened for next week is off. Dr Beeching's plans will go ahead but the unions have received promises from British Railways of better terms for redundancies.

**Saturday 11**  **"Air Fares Battle"** Britain has sent Washington a 'vigorous official Note' protesting at United States policy over transatlantic and transpacific air fares in a last-minute attempt to avoid a major clash which could halt all flights between the two countries.

**Sunday 12**  **"Threat to Atomic Submarines"** The demarcation dispute between electricians and sheet metal workers at the shipyard of Vickers-Armstrongs in Barrow, flared up when 60 electricians were dismissed for refusing to work on the trunking of electric cables on the frigate Mohawk.

**Monday 13**  **"President Kennedy Sends Troops to Birmingham, Alabama"** Houses were bombed, including that of Martin Luther King's brother, in violent rioting over desegregation.

### HERE IN BRITAIN

#### "Slim Chance Comes Off"

A slim forger escaped this week from jail, through a 10" x 15" hole. Two prison officers stood outside the windowless hospital lavatory where he went inside and *vanished.* He had opened a cupboard door, squeezed through a hole in between the pipes coming up through the floor, dropped 6ft to a ledge below and ran through hospital passages to freedom.

The prisoner had been taken from Pentonville to hospital for treatment to an injured arm. Whilst police searched for him, his brother said, "*he must have lost a lot of weight, last time I saw him he weighed about 14 stone!*"

### AROUND THE WORLD

#### "The French 'Complete Tunnel'"

Details of a new French project for a combined road and rail tunnel under the Channel in the form of a single pre-fabricated concrete tube laid in a trench on the sea bed have been released in Paris.

The tube, prefabricated in sections, would be in oval form, 104ft wide and 39ft high at the centre. It would carry two railway lines with two road lanes 23ft wide down the middle.

Running from the north-east of Dover to Wissant, between Cap Blanc Nez and Gris Nez, it would be 22 miles long, against the 34 miles of the proposed bored railway tunnel.

# WEST END BACK STAGE SQUALOR

More advice for Mrs Worthington was given by the president of Equity when he criticised dirty and insanitary back-stage conditions, saying many West End theatres would be condemned as offices or factories. In at least one central theatre, he said, the actors were provided with little chance of escape in the event of fire. *"There is a fashionable theatre"*, he continued, *"in which the limited air available to the underground dressing rooms passed over an open urinal. For many years, until the gratings at ground level were boarded over, this was used by the customers of a neighbouring public house. Laryngitis was endemic and a throat specialist became almost a permanent member of the staff."*

Then he turned to the matter of washing. Most actors have to use greasepaint or blacking on their faces and bodies. *"In how many theatres can this be removed in a bath-tub or shower? A basin and bucket are all I have ever been offered."* and he quoted one manager as saying *'my girls came to the theatre to dance, not to bathe'.* The attitude being that *'space occupied by a bath could be made to seat two paying spectators.'* Theatres were not the only offenders. Although many facilities were provided at the BBC's new television centre, rehearsals were still conducted in any sort of unoccupied building. During a recent cold spell one production was rehearsed in a hall where the oil-stoves and plumbing broke down and normal toilet facilities for the cast of 70 was dependent on the charity of neighbours. *"If the cast had been making motor cars"*, he said, *"there would have been a three-week strike."*

It seemed that the association would have to black-list theatres in categories like 'Dirty', 'Insanitary' and 'Black Holes of Calcutta'. Managers would be warned that only certain types of production would be executed by Equity members

# MAY 14TH - 20TH 1963

## IN THE NEWS

**Tuesday 14**  **"Greville Wynne Sentenced in Moscow"** Convicted of spying, the Briton was sentenced to eight years in prison and Russia declared personae non grata, several British and American diplomatists mentioned as contacts in his espionage trial.

**Wednesday 15** **"US Gives Way on Air Fares"** The US capitulated before determined British diplomatic pressure, and the threat to detain American airliners, and informed Pan American Airways and Trans World Airlines that they could increase transatlantic air fares as agreed by the International Air Transport Association.

**Thursday 16** **"Chief Enaharo Deported"** After a six month battle to obtain political refuge in Britain, the Chief, who is facing charges of treason in Nigeria where he was leader of the Opposition party, was flown out in a dramatic 1am drama at Gatwick Airport.

**Friday 17**  **"Penkovsky Shot"** Russia announced the execution of Oleg Penkovsky, the Soviet scientist, sentenced to death for passing secrets to Greville Wynne and on to the west.

**Saturday 18**  **"BOAC Trap Gold Gang"** A British security officer who posed as a steward smashed an international, Pakistani gold-smuggling syndicate.

**Sunday 19**  **"Mr Powell Hits at Fluoride Critics"** The Minister of Health referred to 'cranks who are trying to hold up fluoridation of the water supply by scaremongering and misrepresentation'. Around 40 health authorities have now approved the scheme.

**Monday 20**  **"Army Reduces Ever-Ready Target"** The War Office confirmed the planned recruiting figure for the Territorial Army Emergency Reserve - the Ever-readies – has been reduced from 15,000 to 8,000. The reason, regular recruiting is going so well.

## HERE IN BRITAIN

### "Cup Tickets Free"

Spend £50 at Ted Jelly's radio and television shop in Leicester this week and you could win a 7s 6d (37p) FA Cup Final ticket free in the draw. This offer angered local football fans who are clamouring for tickets to see City in this year's Final against Manchester United at Wembley on the 25th but then along came Mr Cory, the scrap dealer, who gave a 7s 6d ticket in exchange for a hundredweight of scrap copper – current value, £7 10s.

Mr Cory, who has never seen a football match quickly disposed of 50 tickets and arranged for another 50 to be delivered!

## AROUND THE WORLD

### "Vive Le Bingo"

Members of Shoreditch and Peckham bingo clubs went for a day out to Boulogne to celebrate the second birthday of their clubs – and what could have been more enjoyable than a couple of hours in the Casino playing bingo? Until the French Ministry clamped down on their plan. Bingo (le loto) is banned in France, but the Brits could have played roulette, boule, baccarat or chemin de fer which *are* allowed in State licensed casinos. Lotteries and horse racing are State monopolies. They enjoyed bingo on the plane to Le Touquet and French customs kept an eye out for illegal 'bingo cards'.

# GLORIOUS SPLASHDOWN

Major Gordon Cooper brought himself and his spacecraft down safely into the Pacific after a voyage of 34hr and 20min through space. He was forced to fire by hand the retrorockets controlling the spacecraft's re-entry to the earth's atmosphere because of a fault in the electrical system. The fault developed during the final stages of his flight of 22 orbits, but the landing was almost exactly on target.

The capsule splashed down less than two miles from the main recovery vessel, a remarkable achievement after a flight of about 575,000 miles at more than 17,000 mph. Major Cooper was directed in the firing of his retrorockets, which slowed down the pace of his flight and brought the capsule back into the earth's atmosphere, by radio by Colonel John Glenn, the first American to orbit the earth and who was stationed in a ship off the south coast of Japan. The exchanges between the two men indicated that the astronaut was handling his emergency operations as coolly as he had performed all his duties throughout his day and a half in space. His Oklahoman drawl betrayed no moment of anxiety at any time during the descent.

A communications blackout happened when the Mercury spacecraft, Faith 7, had passed over Shanghai and re-entered the atmosphere but almost immediately the US aircraft carrier Kearsarge reported that it had picked up the capsule on its radar. Radio communication was quickly re-established with Major Cooper, who reported that the parachute had deployed, that all landing systems were working well, and that he himself was "doing fine". Ten minutes later the parachute and spacecraft were sighted from the deck of the aircraft carrier amid a roar of enthusiasm from the sailors lining the deck, and several helicopters took off for the point of impact to help bring the capsule on board the carrier.

# MAY 21ST - 27TH 1963

## IN THE NEWS

**Tuesday 21**    **"ITV Breakdown Warned"** Associated Television warned shows and jobs were in danger as commercial TV "will cease to exist in its present form" if the government press ahead with their plan to take £18m in tax from ITV's advertising income.

**Wednesday 22**    **"50 MPH Limit at Peak Holiday Weekends"** The speed limit will be imposed this summer on 750 selected miles of trunk roads in England and Wales and will be in force for the five weekends in July and August.

**Thursday 23**    **"Government to Curb Sugar Prices"** A distribution payment would enable housewives to buy sugar at prices well below world prices. Since the beginning of May these have spiralled upward and been reflected to some extent in the shops.

**Friday 24** "    **Fords Strike Looms Closer"** Management told the unions for the last time that they would not employ the 17 men they dismissed for being 'trouble-makers'.

**Saturday 25**    **"£200,000 Bullion Robbery"** Forty bars of gold, valued at £200,000, were stolen by three men from a bullion brokers' warehouse in Paul Street, Finsbury. The thieves loaded the gold into a dark-blue van and escaped into the heavy lunch time traffic.

**Sunday 26**    **"400 Injured in FA Cup Winners Welcome"** In Manchester, about 300,000 people lined the streets to welcome home the winning team. Crowds swept away crush barriers, police and officials.

**Monday 27**    **"African States Unite Against White Rule"** Leaders of 32 African nations have set up an organisation that will give them a united voice for the first time in Africa's history.

## HERE IN BRITAIN

### "Charles Clore Wrong Footed"

The British millionaire 'king' of shoes is not usually tripped up – until he came up against the whims of women. He thought they would flock to buy his new-style square-toe shoes, but instead, they went back to white winklepickers.

In his annual report to the British Shoe Corporation, he admitted heavy losses as the big demand that had been forecast, mainly by fashion writers, never materialised. The result had been "an almost immediate reversion to pointed toes, but with style variations on the winklepicker shoes of 1960 and 1961 plus, in the absence of any strong new trend, many customers 'held back'.

## AROUND THE WORLD

### "Too Short for Long Legs"

A small band of Americans have launched a new crusade. Its leader, a big man as are all his supporters, complains that the American car has grown larger on the outside but smaller inside and that manufacturers should make more roomy cars for bigger people.

Mr Spingarn said he could easily get into the car he bought in 1946, but his new car was almost unenterable for an upright American. *"I intensely dislike creeping into a car like a midnight thief, bowing my head to avoid scraping the roof, and assuming the natal position with my knees under my chin as I drive."*

# A TENNER TO AUSTRALIA

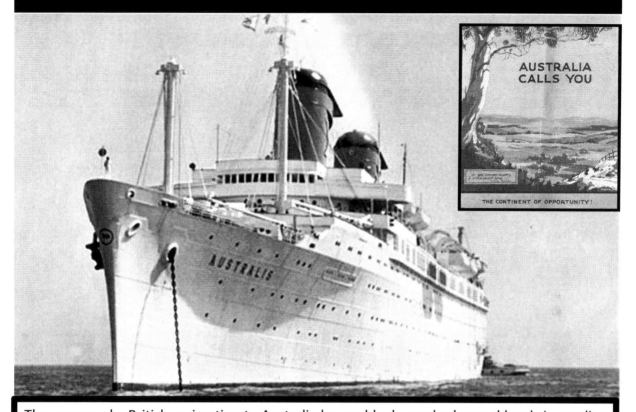

AUSTRALIA CALLS YOU

THE CONTINENT OF OPPORTUNITY!

The reason why British emigration to Australia has suddenly reached record levels is puzzling immigration officials, who announced that 7,040 British immigrants, on the £10 assisted passage scheme, will arrive in Australia this month. This is the largest total for any single month in the past 14 years and there have been 111,000 applications to Australia House in London in the first four months of 1963, more than all last year. Australian immigration officials find their pamphlets have become best sellers in Britain. Each year they give away up to 250,000 copies of each of 12 booklets dealing with aspects of Australian life. The one on housing conditions, which officials said is of interest only to those seriously considering immigration, is being issued at the rate of 28,000 a month.

Experts said no single factor seems to bring about the decision to emigrate but 'opportunity for my children' looms behind many inquiries. Many are motivated by the idea of a classless society in Australia, away from the 'them and us' thinking, in which their children would find it easier to move up the social and work scale than in Britain. White collar workers are among those most influenced along these lines as they appear to feel that in Britain, a child's future is determined too much by the results of the eleven-plus tests.

Other reasons include Britain's severe winter, misgivings about Britain's role in Europe, unemployment, particularly in the north, and indirect publicity for Australia arising from the Commonwealth Games, the royal tour and Test cricket. The most important reason though are success stories from Britons already there. Between 70% and 90% of the new interest arises from reports from relatives and friends. Since 1947 a total of 318,688 Britons have been nominated as immigrants by individuals, mostly by those who went earlier.

## IN THE NEWS

**Tuesday 28**    **"Kenyatta to be Kenya's First Premier"** Jomo Kenyatta is to become prime minister after his party, Kenya African Nation Union, won the country's first general election. Thousands ran through the streets of Nairobi cheering at news.

**Wednesday 29**    **"Homes for the Young at Cost Rents"** As part of their plans to aim at 350,000 new houses a year, the Government put forward schemes to enable younger salaried people and higher wage earners to get houses for 'cost rents' or on a co-ownership basis with housing societies.

**Thursday 30**    **"Help for UK Ship Yards"** The Government are to make £30m available for financing new orders from British owners for ships built in British yards. More money will be provided ' if experience shows that it would be right to do so' until May 31 next year.

**Friday 31**    **"Why No Change in Law"** Angry MPs protested when the Government made it clear they will not introduce a Bill to outlaw racial hatred. The Home Secretary promised instead to step up penalties in the existing law.

**Sat 1 JUNE**    **"Common Market's New Crisis"** Discussions among the Common Market Ministers on regular multilateral exchanges of views between the Six and Britain came to nothing because of opposition by the French.

**Sunday 2**    **"8m Cars Out, Roads Swamped"** All Whit Sunday traffic records were broken with over 150 miles of queues and the new M2 was paralysed.

**Monday 3**    **"Pope John Dies"** Just after a great sunset Mass said for him in St Peter's Square, the 81-year-old Pope's brave suffering came to an end.

### HERE IN BRITAIN

#### "Welsh, but Not Welsh Enough"

Beauty pageant contestant Pat Finch became 'Miss Wales' – but held the crown for just three hours, after which she had to return the silver trophy and the £100 prize money. She was still being congratulated at Rhyl in Flintshire, when she was called before the committee.

The rules are that entrants must be of Welsh nationality, either born in Wales or having lived there for at least 5 years. Pat was born in Blackpool and moved to Wrexham when she was a baby "for some time". The fact that since then she has had a few long holidays in Wales just didn't count!

### AROUND THE WORLD

#### "White Tigers of Rewa for Bristol"

The Maharajah of Rewa has come to a complicated agreement to share four of his eight white tigers with Delhi Zoo if he is allowed to sell a pair of these rare animals to Bristol Zoo for £6,500.

Delhi had suggested the tigers should be given to the nation, but the Maharajah said he would rather destroy them than see the Government get them for nothing.

He will be left with two males and have the right to half of any progeny of the Delhi Zoo tigers. The first female cub born will be his so that he can build up his valuable collection again.

# LIFEBOATMEN ARE SAVIOURS

The International Lifeboat conference took place in Edinburgh and perhaps because lifeboatmen are characteristically unostentatious about their work, maybe because the service they perform makes no financial demands on the ratepayer or taxpayer, many people seem unaware of the hundreds of lives they save each year and the risks and discomfort they undergo. The lifeboat is expected to be at hand when needed, like the police car, the fire engine or the ambulance. That the Royal National Life-boat Institution is supported entirely by voluntary subscriptions probably only occurs to the average person for a few moments a year when he sees a collection box or a poster appealing for funds.

Yet in coastal towns and villages the threat of disaster at sea is more imminent, the lifeboat service is more familiar and volunteers to man the boats continue to come forward and the service is steadily modernising and improving its efficiency with new boats and liaison with other rescue services. A less tangible development in recent years has been the change in the nature of the services the lifeboatmen have been called on to perform. The decline of the fishing industry in many parts of the country has been accompanied by a phenomenal increase in the number of pleasure-boat owners and of 422 lives saved during the year, 232 were in the main holiday months of July, August and September.

As an official put it, the institution's charter is to rescue people from the sea without distinction between nationalities or circumstances and this includes 'bloody fools' as much as those who are victims of an Act of God. A glance at the accounts of rescues in the institution's quarterly journal will convince both the unfortunate and the foolish how great is their debt to those who uncomplainingly risk their lives time and again to save others.

# JUNE 4ᵀᴴ - 10ᵀᴴ 1963

## IN THE NEWS

**Tuesday 4**      **"Queen Recalls the Pope"** Her Majesty recalled the "impressive memories of their meeting with his Holiness in 1961" in her message of condolence to the Vatican.

**Wednesday 5**      **"Seven Cases of Typhoid in Harlow"** With seven confirmed cases and four more suspected, doctors, nurses and public health inspectors were trying to locate the carrier. *"It is like looking for a needle in a haystack",* said one of the team.

**Thursday 6**      **"Profumo Resigns Over Sex Scandal"** Secretary of State for War, John Profumo, resigns from government, admitting he lied *'for the sake of my wife and my family'* to Parliament about his relationship with Christine Keeler.

**Friday 7**      **"Order for All British Satellite"** It was announced at the Paris Air Show that the Government has placed a contract with BAC for the UK3 satellite, due to be launched in three to four years' time.

**Saturday 8**      **"Floods Hit London"** Many parts of London were flooded by heavy rain. The fire brigade received more than 500 calls and in Hendon, police cadets in bathing trunks carried stranded women, through 4ft of water, across the road.

**Sunday 9**      **"Kennedy Tells American Mayors"** Negroes will win their fight and *"It is clear that the time for token moves and idle talk is over, our responsibility is to see that this is won in a peaceful and constructive manner."*

**Monday 10**      **"Ward Charged Over 'Immoral Earnings'"** Dr Stephen Ward, a London osteopath and friend of Christine Keeler, key figures in the Profumo affair, has been charged with living on immoral earnings.

## HERE IN BRITAIN
### "Fireworks in Derby"

At the end of May, thousands of rounds of ammunition exploded in a fire at Derby Drill Hall causing neighbouring houses to be evacuated and police barricades on all roads in the area. A fire officer said, *"When we arrived ammunition was exploding everywhere,"* and a policeman said, *"It was just like a gigantic firework display".*

This week, five minutes after the last of the 120 workers had left for the night from a fireworks factory at Draycott, Derbyshire, there really was a gigantic firework display, when an explosion, followed by fire, destroyed a powder magazine and 10 other buildings.

## AROUND THE WORLD
### "Saved by the Belt"

Three young, French potholers said that chewing a leather belt in place of food helped them to survive five days trapped in a flooded cave. The three dragged themselves to safety, exhausted but uninjured, but they lost two companions who were swept away by a torrent which swirled through the cavern after 60 hours of heavy rain.

The three survivors stumbled, swam and groped their way along ledges to within 50ft of the entrance, but were trapped on a ledge by the rushing waters. On day five, they caught drums containing food, lamps and cigarettes floated down the stream by rescuers.

# COVENTRY CATHEDRAL BUSY

*The Old (right) and New (left) Cathedral Buildings*

The new Coventry cathedral has just celebrated the first anniversary of its consecration service and has had a very busy year. 3.5 million visitors. The day begins with light and silence, a moment for the early Communion service. By 11 o'clock crowds are streaming up the aisles and this goes on all day as up to 20,000 of them pass through the building.

The visitors come from all parts of the country and from overseas, they are of all ages and many religions. By early afternoon on a weekday, there could be a 100-yard queue of them at the cathedral door. Afterwards some will say they loved the building and some that they loathed it. Some visitors write to complain because, for instance, the cathedral was being used by 3,000 Welsh Pilgrims and 2,500 members Of the Church Missionary Society on the afternoon they could not get in. Some 200 people write every day to inquire about visits. Visitors make their donations at the door and scramble for guidebooks in the cathedral bookshop or the overflow on tables in the refectory.

Judged by stately home standards, Coventry Cathedral is a great hit but there is more to it than that. A German Lutheran pastor said, *"At two other English cathedrals we were not allowed into the Communion, but here we could go. Communion in Germany is something rather black and dark but at Coventry it was a gay occasion."* Another said, *"To make a comparison with Canterbury and York, I would say that there were a good many dead bishops lying about in those other places, but no people seemed to be there singing at the services."* At the weekday lunchtime service at Coventry, there were 2,400 people singing to the rafters.

# JUNE 11ᵀᴴ - 17ᵀᴴ 1963

## IN THE NEWS

**Tuesday 11**    **"Mr K Agrees to Test Ban Talks"** Mr Khrushchev, President Kennedy and the Prime Minister, have agreed to send representatives to a meeting in Moscow in July.

**Wednesday 12** **"Negro Students Enrol in Alabama"** Federal troops enforced the desegregation of the University of Alabama after defiant opposition from George Wallace, the State Governor. The two students went in after orders from President Kennedy.

**Thursday 13**    **"Warm Welcome for India's President"** With the full ceremonial of a state visit to London, the Queen and the Duke of Edinburgh greeted Dr Radhakrishnan who is making a 12-day tour of Britain.

**Friday 14**    **"British Troops in Swaziland"** A battalion of the 1st Gordon Highlanders left Nairobi, Kenya, at the request of the Swaziland authorities to assist the police force in maintaining order during a general strike, which has been going on since May 20.

**Saturday 15**    **"Last Night at the Old Vic"** The Old Vic Company held the last performance of the company, Shakespeare's 'Measure for Measure'. The new National Theatre Company will be based in the theatre until its new premises are built.

**Sunday 16**    **"Soviets Launch First Woman into Space"** Lieutenant Valentina Tereshkova, a former textile worker, has become the first woman in space in her spaceship Vostok VI.

**Monday 17**    **"British Fighter Crashes at Paris Air Show"** One of the two Hawker PI 127 vertical take-off and landing fighters crashed while being demonstrated on the final day of the Paris air show. The chief test pilot was uninjured.

## HERE IN BRITAIN

### "Unhappy Campers"

Scores of angry holidaymakers packed into a hall to demand a refund from Pontins. The unhappy campers at Christchurch, Hampshire, complained that when they arrived, the amenity building containing a ballroom, restaurant and bar was still under construction.

There were ants in the chalets, a bus cost 1s 6d, three hours' television cost 2s and electricity was 4d a unit. The statement from Management said, "We slipped up. We admit that. Alternative arrangements have been made, free coach trips and free facilities for tennis have been laid on and every effort is being made to give everybody a happy holiday."

## AROUND THE WORLD

### "$1,000 Not to Use My Train"

The owner of a local railway in New Jersey has offered each of the 200 regular passengers who commute daily, $1,000 (£357) in cash if they will stop using his trains for the 36 miles to work.

He bought the New York, Susquehanna and Western Railroad last month and said the alternative is a reduced service of one train a day in each direction instead of three. The passenger service is uneconomic and he wants to concentrate on goods services. Few are considering the offer. It is not enough to make up for the inconvenience if they went by car or bus.

# SEAGULL ORBITS THE EARTH

On June 16, 1963 **Valentina Tereshkova** became the first woman in space

# THE FIRST WOMAN IN SPACE

She was
born in 1937

The spaceship:
**Vostok VI**

Chaika (seagull)
was her call sign

Completed 48
orbits of the Earth—
**20,11,680 km**
—in two days,
22 hours and 50
minutes

Various locations &
monuments have
been named after
her

❝ *Once you've been in space,*
*you appreciate how small*
*and fragile the Earth is* ❞

The first ever woman cosmonaut, Valentina Tereshkova, was launched into space and, when, whilst circling the world at 18,000 miles an hour, listeners in Moscow heard 'Seagull's' excited voice say, *"I see the earth ...I feel excellent"*, excitement reached a pitch not known since the Soviet Union shook the world with the launching of the first space man, Yuri Gagarin, in 1961. Official announcements began pouring out on Miss Tereshkova, a former textile worker and expert parachutist.

Yet, why not a woman in space? The so-called weaker sex long ago proved their durability. They fly jet planes, they do dare-devil circus acts and they have babies – still one of the toughest physical and emotional tests of all. According to a Las Vegas club owner, who has studied the question for years, women are luckier than men too – and they live longer. A medical adviser who helps select American *male* astronauts sees no reason why women should not be shot into space. They have passed the tough medical tests and could have an advantage, they eat less and use less oxygen and it hardly matters, when weightless, if they are smaller and weaker. Mentally too, women may have the edge, as one of the strains on an astronaut is loneliness and women are generally better conditioned to this than men. They are used to it. It has been shown that women have just as good endurance as men, they stand up well to hard conditions and, as one woman mountaineer says, they cope better with unexpected shocks.

The Russians want to know if there is any difference for men and women in space and whether radiation will affect a woman's chances of having babies. If the dreams of planting human colonies on the moon are ever to be realised, this question needs to be answered.

# JUNE 18TH - 24TH 1963

## IN THE NEWS

**Tuesday 18**    **"Lords Prayer Banned in US Schools"** The Supreme Court set off a bitter controversy by ruling that the use of the Prayer and the Bible at devotional exercises in state-supported schools was unconstitutional.

**Wednesday 19**    **"Cassius Does it in Five"** Although he'd been knocked down in the 4th round, the "Louisville Lip" stopped Britain's Henry Cooper in the 5th round as he'd predicted, when Henry suffered a severely cut eye.

**Thursday 20**    **"Russian Space Record"** The Russian astronauts have landed safely in central Asia. Colonel Bykovsky set a new Soviet record by staying in orbit for more than four days.

**Friday 21**    **"Sweeping Plans for Civil Rights"** President Kennedy outlined the most sweeping civil rights legislation of the century including seeking rights for individuals claiming discrimination in schools, restaurants, shops and hotels.

**Saturday 22**    **"Pope Paul VI"** The smoke from the chimney of the Sistine Chapel was unquestionably white and a vast crowd acclaimed the new Pope when the former Cardinal Montini, Archbishop of Milan, made his appearance on the central balcony of St Peter's.

**Sunday 23**    **"A Rousing German Welcome"** Hundreds of thousands of waving and cheering people gave President Kennedy a hero's welcome in Cologne and Bonn. They greeted him as a friend to whom they knew they owed their life and liberty.

**Monday 24**    **"Five Britons Killed in Yemen"** Five British soldiers were killed when a party of British Service personnel from Aden, including eight women, lost their way on an 'Adventure Training' exercise and inadvertently walked into hostile Yemen territory.

## HERE IN BRITAIN

### "Charles and that Cherry Brandy"

Buckingham Palace admitted the Prince of Wales did visit the bar of a Stornoway hotel and pay 2s 6d for a cherry brandy before dinner. He had gone to the Isle of Lewis on a trip round the coast of Scotland with a party from his Gordonstoun school on their training ship 'Pinta'.

That evening he was taken to the Crown Hotel for a meal with four other boys – but before the meal, he nipped into the cocktail bar!

Alcohol is strictly against the rules. The Prince then went with the others to see a Jayne Mansfield film – but that *was* within the rules.

## AROUND THE WORLD

### "Suspense at the Vatican"

The keys turned on the Sacred College of Cardinals as the princes of the Roman Church were cut off from direct worldly contact while they decided which one of them should be Pope. The suspense is felt by more than the Roman Catholic faithful or even the 'bookies'. There is, formality and history, uncertainty, controversy and real power, combined with invocations of the super-natural.

The proceedings reach their culmination when, after balloting, discussion and praying, all the cardinals but one lower the canopies above their stalls, indicating that they are no longer the equals of the man whom they have just elected.

The Thames Barge sailing race was held for the last time this month. This is the centenary year of the match and the idea of the first race was entirely due to Henry Dodd, a refuse contractor immortalised by Dickens as 'Noddy' Boffin, the Golden Dustman, in 'Our Mutual Friend'. A self-made man in the true Victorian tradition, he was born in 1801 starting life as a plough boy. In his early twenties he began organising the rubbish collections of London working as a 'scavenger' sorting 'rough stuff' as it was known. He discovered that he could make more money moving it, rather than sorting it, so from horse-drawn carts he expanded into Spritsail Sailing Barges to deliver the refuse to works on the shores of the Thames Estuary.

The first race, organised under the auspices of the Prince of Wales Yacht Club, (the name assumed from the pub where the members met!) took place in August 1863. Eight barges took part including Dodd's own, the WHD, who triumphed and was first home. Dodd died in 1881 and left funds from his considerable estate, £100,000, to sustain the Match. He also left £5,000 to the Fishmongers Company, the interest to support poor bargemen.

For the Centenary Match, the two principal rivals in Britain's coasting trade, F T Everard and The London & The Rochester Trading Co, lavished money on their fastest barges. The 48-mile course was from Mucking to the Mouse Lightship and back up to Gravesend. F T Everard's 'Veronica' was the winner, leaving the rest far behind in her wake. The original challenge cup was lost at the beginning of this century, but the present one, the Will. Everard memorial gold cup was presented first to the owners of 'Veronica' and then to the National Maritime Museum.

# JUNE 25TH - JULY 1ST 1963

## IN THE NEWS

**Tuesday 25**     **"Light and Airy Paddington"** Paddington station has been repainted and its vast glass roof cleaned. Two 24-hour cipher clocks have been installed and others given sub-titles from 13 to 0 to bring them into line.

**Wednesday 26**     **"£2.5m to Double Gatwick Terminal"** A contract for extensions and to add a third passenger pier by the summer of 1965 was announced by the Minister of Aviation.

**Thursday 27**     **"Darlin' Welcome for JFK in Ireland"** The US President received a rapturous welcome on an emotional visit to his ancestral homeland in County Wexford on the second day of his four-day trip to Ireland.

**Friday 28**     **"Inquiry into Yemen Incident"** A joint Services board of inquiry began into the incident in which four British servicemen were killed by Yemeni tribesmen. Eighteen British servicemen are still held by the Yemenis but are reported to be safe and well.

**Saturday 29**     **"£300m Oil Boom"** Two giants of Britain's oil industry, BP and Shell, have made a take-over bid for a third, the Burmah Oil Company which puts a value of £300m on Burmah.

**Sunday 30**     **"Splendour of Pope Paul's Coronation"** St. Peter's Square provided a scene of grandeur as vast crowds, estimated at over 300,000, gathered under the hot setting sun to watch the ceremony and the Papal Mass.

**Monday July 1**     **"The Stephen Ward Trial"** Witness Marilyn 'Mandy' Rice-Davies, in response to learning of a denial from Lord Astor that they had a sexual relationship, responded with the phrase, *"He would, wouldn't he."*

---

## HERE IN BRITAIN

### "That Just Wasn't Cricket"

Millions were watching the exciting climax of the Second Test match. England needed 12 runs to win with two wickets to fall and only seven minutes left … *the BBC faded out the match to put on the scheduled 5.50pm News bulletin!* Within seconds, angry viewers were telephoning and after only two minutes, they saw the announcer take a telephone call and say, *"We are going straight back to Lord's"* The speed was due to a call from Head of BBC Presentation, *a keen cricketer!* Alas, the match ended in a draw with England still six runs from victory with one wicket left.

## AROUND THE WORLD

### "Kennedy: 'Ich bin ein Berliner'"

The US President, John F Kennedy, made a ground-breaking speech in Berlin offering American solidarity to the citizens of West Germany. A crowd of 120,000 Berliners had gathered in the square outside City Hall long before he was due to arrive, and when he finally appeared on the podium, gave him an ovation of several minutes.

The president had just returned from a visit on foot to Checkpoint Charlie, where he was watched from the other side of the border by small groups of East Berliners unable even to wave because of the huge numbers of the East German People's Police.

# UNWILLING CUSTODIANS

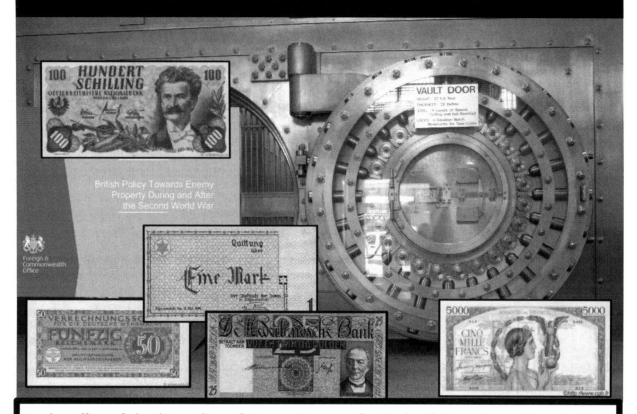

In the office of the 'Custodian of Enemy Property for England' the strings of hundreds of human stories from WW2 are laboriously tied together. Immediately after the war, the department's main task was to collate property and cash, stocks and shares which had been owned by Germans, Italians, Japanese and other 'belligerents', and which had remained here at the outbreak of war in 1939. This work is now virtually complete, most of the assets having gone in reparations to British citizens.

A smaller group, the 'non-belligerents', from countries with whom Britain was not at war but who were overrun by the Axis are proving much more difficult to sort out. Unlike the 'belligerents' they are still 'individuals' and as such are entitled to claim any money they had deposited here, be that 2s or £100,000. Almost £2m is still held and every year between 300 and 400 claims come in from all over the world. Accompanying the claims are human stories, all of which must be validated to the satisfaction of the men who run the department with shrewdness tempered with benevolence. Among them is a treasury of detailed knowledge of Europe between 1939 and 1945.

In Belgium, the Netherlands, Denmark and Norway, most of the claimants, or their heirs, have been traced. The French have had less success, but the department's biggest difficulty is the money and stock owned by people living behind the iron curtain. Many of these know that their money is locked up in London but neither side can do anything about it. And the eventual disposal of some assets poses a question to which the Government has no answer yet. This is the money deposited for safe keeping and in high hope for the future and whose owners' human stories ended, not happily, but tragically, in places like Dachau, Buchenwald and Belsen.

# JULY 2ND - 8TH 1963

## IN THE NEWS

**Tuesday 2**    **"Harold 'Kim" Philby the Third Man"** It was confirmed that the Foreign Office official who disappeared from Beirut four months ago, warned the spies Burgess and Maclean in time for them to escape to Russia.

**Wednesday 3**    **"Khrushchev Offers Test-Ban Treaty"** The Soviet leader offered to conclude a separate treaty on the banning of nuclear tests in the atmosphere, space and under water. He did not include under-ground testing.

**Thursday 4**    **"More Troops for British Guiana"** Troops from the 2nd Battalion of the Green Jackets have been flown to assist the government in Georgetown which is suffering riots and violence during a protracted general strike.

**Friday 5**    **"Captive Britons Returned"** The remaining 16 men of the British group of service men and women who blundered into Yemen territory 11 days ago have been returned to Aden. The Yemen Foreign Ministry has accepted the promise of 'a sum' of money'.

**Saturday 6**    **"Chinese Arrive in Moscow"** The Chinese delegation for the ideological talks with Russia were greeted with cheers from the staff of the Chinese Embassy and students. The Russians offered handshakes and beaming smiles, but no Soviet press were present.

**Sunday 7**    **"Britons Die in Autobahn Crash"** Six British tourists died and many more were injured when their coach plunged over a bridge and fell 45ft to a railway line.

**Monday 8**    **"Renewed Drive Against the Mafia"** Italy is gripped by one of their periodic spasms of determination to challenge the Sicilian Mafia in the wake of the deaths a week ago of seven policemen and soldiers killed by a booby-trap near Palermo.

## HERE IN BRITAIN

### "Horror Cards in Sweets"

The Minister of Education said he was powerless to suppress the production or distribution of picture cards enclosed packets of chewing gum. The horror cards show scenes of bestiality as Martians invade the earth. A set of 55 depict hideous creatures in space helmets committing gruesome acts and bear such titles as 'Destroying a dog'; 'Removing the victims' and 'Burning flesh'. On the back of the cards is a worded description.

A headmaster of a junior school who found the cards circulating among his pupils, said, *"I've never seen anything so terrifying. These cards are the vilest I have come across."*

## AROUND THE WORLD

### "Troops Fire on British Guiana Crowds"

British troops, called in to break up race riots in British Guiana opened fire after repeated warnings had been ignored. Two men were shot dead and two others wounded by a detachment of the Coldstream Guards before order was restored. Large numbers of Guyanese of East Indian and Negro descent had been fighting with a variety of weapons, including knives, bottles and clubs.

An agreement to end the strike, which has crippled the colony for more than 11 weeks, was prepared by Bob Willis the British TUC representative and signed later that night by the Premier, Dr Jagan and the Guiana TUC.

# SIGNS OF THE TIMES

The Traffic Signs Committee propose that Britain's system of traffic signs should be replaced by a Continental-styled one, using mainly symbols instead of words. *"We believe",* the committee say, *"that our existing traffic signs are seriously out-of-date in relation to the present and foreseeable numbers and speeds of vehicles".* For the ordinary motorist the most important advance under the committee's proposals will be towards clarity and away from the reading or interpretation of words and letters of varying type. The committee say that 'Halt' and 'Slow' signs should be replaced by 'Stop' and 'Give Way' - the 'Give Way' sign being mandatory and to be used on all minor roads at junctions with primary routes in rural areas.

The old signs and their new replacements

Among the new signs, 'Turn Right', 'Turn Left', and 'Keep Left' would be indicated by white arrows on blue discs. For 'No Right', 'No Left', or 'No U-turn', the committee recommend the Continental red-and-black cancelled symbol signs. 'No Entry' would be shown by a white bar on a red disc, 'No Overtaking' by the Continental two-car silhouette with a cancelled symbol and one-way traffic by a simple system of arrows.

Since half the fatal or serious accidents occur at or near junctions, the committee say that minor and major roads should be very clearly distinguished by new, emphatic carriageway markings at the mouths of minor roads - a transverse, double broken white line half-way across and a longitudinal white warning line down the centre of 'the minor road'.

# JULY 9TH - 15TH 1963

## IN THE NEWS

**Tuesday 9**  "The Riddle of Rachman" Bizarre questions arising from testimony by 'Mandy' Rice Davies in the Stephen Ward case, were asked in the Commons by a London MP. Did the property racketeer really die last November or was there a switch of bodies?

**Wednesday 10**  "Fights in Whitehall" As the King and Queen of Greece dined at Buckingham Palace, police fought a running battle in Whitehall with black sashed members of the 'Committee of 100' protesting at the alleged confinement in Greece of political prisoners.

**Thursday 11**  "Recruiting Slump for Army" A sharp drop in numbers has shocked the War Office planners who are aiming to build up a 180,000 strong Army by next April. The enlistments have declined following measures to restrict recruits mainly to single men.

**Friday 12**  "Soviet Agent Flees to West" An important Russian agent, described as 'very, very important" has arrived in Britain via the US. He is being guarded by MI5 at a secret hide-out and remains anonymous as his life may be in danger

**Saturday 13**  "Rioting in Maryland" The Governor of Mississippi said in testimony to Congress that the Kennedy brothers' civil rights legislation was sowing seeds of hate and violence that could lead to a 'bloody harvest'.

**Sunday 14**  "Foreign Legion Steals the Show" Large crowds watched the traditional Bastille Day military parade and fly-past in on the Champs Elysees. Many felt the show was stolen by the impressive stroll-like march past of the Foreign Legion, back on parade for the first time since the 1961 Algiers uprising.

**Monday 15**  "All Smiles in Moscow" Mr Khrushchev led the Soviet Union negotiators when the nuclear test-ban talks with Britain and America opened.

## HERE IN BRITAIN

### "Hoverbus Service on the Thames"

A revolutionary transport service started on the Thames with the Denny D2 Hoverbus carrying up to 70 passengers on trips from the Festival Hall pier up-river as far as the Houses of Parliament and downstream to Tower Bridge. Able to travel at 21 knots, this 831ft-long Hovercraft is stable and virtually noiseless but does create significant wash and spray.

But it might have a problem with driftwood as its rudder propeller is under the stern. Power to the air cushion will have to be cut when an obstacle is spotted letting the Hovercraft float on the surface until the way is clear.

## AROUND THE WORLD

### "Hedge-Hop to Freedom"

A Polish air force officer hedge-hopped 170 miles with his wife and children in a training plane in the first ever escape flight to West Berlin. He flew at 150ft the whole time to avoid radar and make it impossible for jet planes to intercept him without endangering themselves. He took off in the two-seater plane from Nadarzyce in Poland after getting permission to fly east. Instead he reduced his height and turned west, landing at Tempelhof airport in the American sector. Even his family did not know of his plan, his wife thought they were going to visit relatives in Stettin, East Germany, when they took off.

# Pearl Fishing

For more than 4,000 years, pearl fleets have left Bahrain each spring to spend three months on the pearl oyster beds of the Persian Gulf. Only 30 years ago, 500 ships carrying 20,000 men sailed from Bahrain. This year no more than 12 boats with fewer than 1,000 men. Falling demand for natural pearls and competition from the cheaper, cultured pearl, has caused a decline in the industry and gone are the days of pearls as large as olives!

In the early morning, an overpowering stench fills the air of oysters which have been collected and left overnight to allow their muscles to relax and which lie, ankle deep, on the decks of the boats waiting to be opened with curved blunt knives. If a pearl is found, it is placed on the finder's foot, or between his toes and when several pearls have been collected, they are handed to the captain for storage in his brass-studded chest. The divers claim they find one pearl, most tiny seed pearls, to every five oysters. A pearl the size of a pea is a prize!

That day's diving then begins. A diver slips over the side and 'stands' in the water on a heavy weight tied to the end of a long rope held by the 'puller' on the boat. He holds a string bag attached to the end of a second rope, clips a bone peg on his nose, takes a deep breath and is quickly lowered into the depths by the 'puller'. On the seabed he releases the weight and scours the bottom searching for oysters. After about two minutes he tugs the rope and is drawn up quickly by his 'puller'. Each team makes from 15 to 20 dives and a diver will, perhaps, earn £50 for his months of toil.

# JULY 16TH - 22ND 1963

## IN THE NEWS

**Tuesday 16** **"Test Ban Negotiations Start Well"** Mr. Khrushchev got the talks with America and Britain off to a good start. He jokingly asked at the beginning of the 3½ hour opening session, *"Shall we start off by signing the agreement right away?"*

**Wednesday 17** **"Jackpot Order for Jet"** Britain's new BAC One-Eleven jetliner has won a £14m order from the giant American Airlines.

**Thursday 18** **"Slump Hits Steel Men"** 4,000 steel workers in south Wales will be put on short time working because of a shortage of orders from the motor industry and tinplate works.

**Friday 19** **"Measles Vaccine for Britain"** Mr Powell, Minister of Health, announced that large-scale production of measles vaccine was under way in Britain, but he would not recommend its general use until he had been given the 'all clear'.

**Saturday 20** **"Slum Rent Racketeers"** Scotland Yard are investigating scores of complaints from people claiming to be victims of 'Rachman type' landlords who employ gangsters called the 'Heavy Glove Men' to terrorise tenants.

**Sunday 21** **"Museums and Galleries Shut by Strike Pickets"** The Tower of London and British Museum were among 21 museums and art galleries closed to the public for 24 hours because of a dispute over pay and hours by the 'Beefeaters'.

**Monday 22** **"The Ice-Cold War"** Banging of gongs and drums in Peking marks the final split between Russia and China after the failure of their talks on 'ideological differences'.

---

### HERE IN BRITAIN

**"Experts Baffled by Crater"**

A crater in a field at Charlton Donhead in Dorset, had Army bomb disposal experts baffled and some local villagers suggesting that it was made by a spacecraft. As police kept the public away from the field, experts were trying to establish what happened to the potatoes and barley that had been growing where the 8ft wide crater was found and what happened to the cow found in a field near by with its hide peeling in scales as though it had been scorched.

The potatoes and barley had completely disappeared. Captain John Rogers, leader of the Army team said, *"I am completely baffled"*.

### AROUND THE WORLD

**"Tax-Free Snow for Switzerland"**

The Swiss Government ruled today that snow and water may be imported tax-free to Switzerland. This 'coals to Newcastle' decision was to clear up doubts of conscientious customs men on the French border who never knew whether duty charges should apply to snow and water.

Switzerland, the home of winter sports, really does need foreign snow on occasions. Resorts near the French border sometimes import it to prepare ski jumps when the weather delays the start of the winter season. Large quantities of water were brought in from France to supply parched villages in the Jura Mountains last summer, which was exceptionally dry.

# TOTAL ECLIPSE OF THE SUN

*The Total Eclipse of 1963 Near Cadillac Mountain, Maine.*

Scientists photographed the total eclipse of the sun over north America from jet aircraft travelling along the path of the moon's shadow. The eclipse was observed from northern Japan, across Alaska, Canada and Maine until it was lost in the Atlantic. On Cadillac Mountain, 20 scientific teams plus 2,000 or 3,000 holiday makers had an almost perfect view. This phenomenon is likely to occur only once in 360 years in any one place on the earth's surface and if missed, the next chance of seeing a total eclipse in any part of Maine will be May 1, 2079.

At dawn the mountain top was busy. Telescopes were carefully balanced on the irregular pink granite, cardboard boxes were fashioned into pinhole viewers, chairs set up, cameras adjusted, and transistor radios tuned in to a commentary. Then there was coolness in the air and in the north-west, a black shadow seemed to hover over the ground before racing towards the mountain and enveloping it in darkness. All round, the horizon brightness crept through, as if from under a closed door, and sped eastward at more than 3,000mph. It came to Cadillac Mountain simultaneously with the crack of a jet aircraft breaking the sound barrier trying to keep up.

There was some reluctance to watch the eclipse, possibly because of the warnings about eye damage broadcast repeatedly. Authorities received several telephone calls. One from a woman wanting to know what kind of protection she should have to watch the eclipse on television. A second from a farmer wanting to know if it was safe to leave the cows out. A third who rang several hours after the eclipse to find out if she could let the children out of the house. One irate woman demanded to know *'why, if it were so dangerous to watch, were they holding an eclipse at all!'*

# JULY 23RD - 29TH 1963

## IN THE NEWS

**Tuesday 23**    **"Sizzling London Feels the Bite"** 79.3 deg Fahrenheit, (26C), the hottest day since September 1961, brought a plague of gnats in the evening causing thousands misery with their bites.

**Wednesday 24**    **"A New Queen"** The Government is to provide financial assistance towards a replacement for the liner Queen Mary. The Cunard Steam-Ship Company is believed to have decided on a liner of 55,000 tons at an estimated cost of more than £20m.

**Thursday 25**    **"Ward Art Show to Quit"** The gallery owners exhibiting the paintings of Stephen Ward now on trial at the Old Bailey, has been given a 'notice of closure' on the grounds of 'breaking a local by-law'.

**Friday 26**    **"A Great Day for World Peace"** Russia, the United States and Britain initialled a treaty to ban all nuclear tests except those underground. The initialling was done by Mr. Gromyko (Russia), Mr. Averell Harriman (United States) and Lord Hailsham (Britain) and *'will be signed at a date convenient to all'*.

**Saturday 27**    **"Thousands Killed in Yugoslav Earthquake"** 10,000 people feared dead after a massive earthquake rocked the Yugoslav city of Skopje. The quake occurred in the Macedonian capital and tremors were felt some 90 miles along the Vardar valley.

**Sunday 28**    **"President Appeals to France"** President Kennedy said in a broadcast that the nuclear test ban agreement was a victory for mankind and made a direct appeal to President de Gaulle to sign the treaty and abandon the French nuclear testing programme.

**Monday 29**    **"Mr Marples' 50 mph"** The first weekend 'try-out' of the national speed-limit was deemed a failure! It was ignored by many motorists and is impossible to enforce.

### HERE IN BRITAIN
#### "Motorway Speed Limit Proposed"

The designer of Britain's newest motorway, the Preston to Warrington section of the M6 said he would like to see a speed limit imposed as they have in America. *"The road is built for speeds up to 70 mph and because of the narrow central reservation it would be better if that was the maximum permitted speed."* He added, *"I am not worried about the 100- mph man killing himself, but if he gets a tyre burst, he may cross to the other carriageway and kill other people."* He also thought that there should be a minimum speed limit of 40 mph.

### AROUND THE WORLD
#### "Scowling Liston Weighs-In"

Sonny Liston was fined $100 for being late at the weigh-in for his title fight with Floyd Patterson. He got a slow hand clap and boos from the impatient crowd in Las Vegas. Liston who won the world heavyweight championship from Patterson on a one-round knock-out last September, put on a big scowl for everyone in the Convention Hall and glared fiercely across the scales at Patterson, who met his gaze. Then he looked away - *and winked at his friends!* Liston frequently uses the 'stare' technique to try to scare his opponents! He later retained his title by scoring a second first-round knockout.

# 'PETTICOAT RULE'

A survey, conducted by 'The Times', of 29 city and town councils and one county council of varied political complexions, has revealed that an average of one in seven local councillors is described as 'retired' and that one in nine is a housewife and one might wonder if this is because of a consuming urge to make our town a better place or a desire to occupy increased leisure time now that the children are off their hands and the daily trek to office and factory is over?

Trailing behind these two groups come Company directors (one in 13), trade union officials (one in 32), solicitors and barristers (one in 35), builders and contractors (one in 52) and estate agents and surveyors (one in 68). Heading the petticoat regimes were Newcastle upon Tyne and Southampton, with a ratio of one housewife to every five members on the councils. Oxfordshire County Council led the way with 'retired' representation, with 18 out of 64. In Cardiff, the lawyers (nine) are almost as numerous as the housewives (10); and Leeds (11) and Liverpool (12) are particularly well off for trade union officials.

A combination of the figures for builders, contractors, estate agents, architects and various builders' merchants, shows that one in every 25 councillors has a direct or indirect interest in the sale or use of land. They become the largest trade and professional group in local government. With so much power over building and land use-road improvements, housing, schools and hospitals resting in local councils these councillors are faced with more frequent conflicts of loyalty than their colleagues. A committee chairman in a large urban authority said, *"Unquestionably it is helpful to a surveyor or a builder to serve on a local council. Even if they are not serving on a planning committee, they cannot help hearing things".*

## IN THE NEWS

**Tuesday 30**    **"Rail Closures 'Stampede' Feared"** The Government and British Railways were accused of withholding information about proposed line closures, deliberately reducing earnings and keeping costs at a high level to enable them to present a better case for closures.

**Wednesday 31** **"The Traitors' Reunion"** Harold 'Kim' Philby has been granted asylum in Russia and given Soviet citizenship. He is together again with Burgess and Maclean in Moscow.

**Thurs 1 Aug**    **"Dr Ward Guilty – Suicide"** In the "Profumo affair", the Old Bailey jury found Stephen Ward guilty of living on immoral earnings by which time he had already taken an overdose of barbiturates.

**Friday 2**    **"Malta Independent by May"** The 'George Cross Island' is to become independent not later than May 31, 1964. This was the only concrete decision to emerge from the Malta independence conference, which ended in disorder.

**Saturday 3**    **"Hanratty Rightly Convicted"** The Home Secretary refused to set up a public inquiry into the A6 murder case, the crime for which James Hanratty was convicted and hanged in April last year.

**Sunday 4**    **"The Bank Holiday Getaway"** A 'day of the missing millions' was the AA's report on a dull and drizzly Bank holiday Sunday which followed one of the wettest August Bank holiday Saturdays for several years. But at London Airport one passenger every three seconds was passing through at peak times.

**Monday 5**    **"US Retaliation in European Chicken War"** Some US tariff concessions will be withdrawn following the introduction of high Common Market duties on American chicken. US chicken sales have dropped by £16m a year.

### HERE IN BRITAIN

#### "The Profumo By-Election"

Nomination papers for the Stratford by-election were posted to HM Prison, Hull as requested by Herbert Lawrence Stratton, prisoner No 1839. Stratton stated that he wished to stand as a candidate and pointed out that he was in prison for a misdemeanour, not a felony, which meant he was eligible. If he is to fight the election from his cell, Stratton faces perhaps insuperable difficulties before nominations close on August 3rd. He must find a deposit of £150; must be proposed and seconded by local electors and his nomination papers must be signed by eight other people who have the right to vote.

### AROUND THE WORLD

#### "No Music in Capri"

The municipal authorities of Capri have issued an order banning transistor radios, record players and juke boxes, not only on the island's beaches, but in the public squares of the town itself. The habit is getting out of hand. Swimmers keep close to rocks rather than pushing out to sea so they can remain in range of the little wireless placed on the end of the promontory. There will be interest to see if this initiative is followed elsewhere in Italy. Unsuccessful attempts at reducing noise include a ban on motor scooters in the centre of Florence and the imposition of fines.

# LEFT HANDED? LEFT OUT!

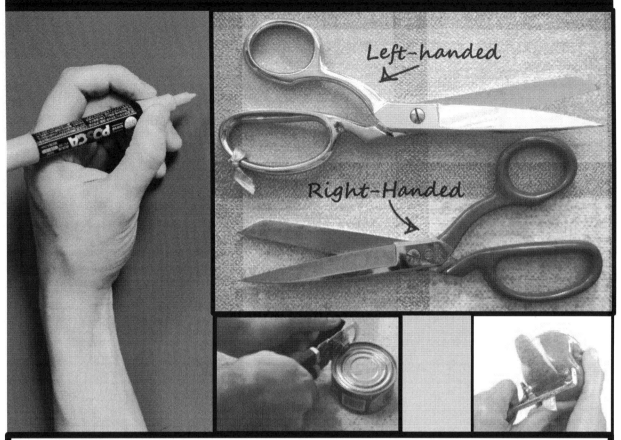

Left-handed

Right-Handed

The sad history of the left-handed schoolchild being rapped across the knuckles is fortunately a fading one, but the minor irritations that accompany the 'handicap' can last a lifetime for some women. If being left-handed is a drawback to earning your living, ways and means are soon found to put that right, as builders' tools are all made for right and left-handed users and are easily obtained.

In the home, the picture is less bright. Dressmaking shears are painful to hold because the slanting edge on the finger holes dig into your fingers. The handle of the wall tin opener must be operated with the weaker hand. *"Little inconveniences"*, a left-handed housewife said, *"hardly worth making a fuss about, but I do wonder sometimes why the manufacturer who says he is 'so anxious to please' can't do just a little more for us"*.

*"We do have inquiries from left-handed people"*, said a scissors manufacturer, *"but they are very few and far between. Only a person like a left-handed tailor, using scissors all day long, would be likely to complain and few manufacturers would risk stamping left-handed scissors for that small market."* A manufacturer of secateurs, on the other hand, said that they could be used equally well either way and that thought was given to this at the designing stage.

Only one kitchen implement was absolutely useless to the left-handed housekeeper, the product planning department of a highly reputable firm pointed out. That was the potato peeler and they produced this and the conventional type of tin opener, for both the left and right-handed markets and handles on their saucepans, the spokesman added, were cunningly contrived to suit either grip. *"Left handers do get a reasonable crack at the whip when it comes to household products"*, he said, *"I know because I am one - and a bachelor."*

# IN THE NEWS

**Tuesday 6**   **"Chaos at Hiroshima Peace Rally"** The 9th World Congress against Atomic and Hydrogen Bombs was in tatters before it had even started as factions struggled for control and the Russians turned their backs on the Chinese speaker.

**Wednesday 7**   **"Finland Hails Mr Macmillan's Visit"** This first visit by a British Prime Minister is using the impetus of its treaty with Russia to increase trade and cooperation..

**Thursday 8**   **"Mail Train Robbery"** The Royal Mail train from Glasgow to Euston was stopped by armed robbers at Sears Crossing near Linslade in Buckinghamshire. It is thought up to £2.5m is stolen and it triggers the biggest detective hunt in history.

**Friday 9**   **"A Bed for 3s in Latest BR Ship"** Travellers can find a first-class bed for 3s (15p) a night on the SS Avalon on the BR Harwich-Hook of Holland service. Prices, on top of the fares, start from 3s for a berth, complete with sheets, pillowcases, blankets and towel.

**Saturday 10**   **"Chaos as Night Fire Closes Waterloo"** A small, quickly extinguished fire damaged signalling wires and points motors, cancelled many trains and delayed thousands.

**Sunday 11**   **"Footplate Fight in Great Train Robbery"** The injured driver of the Glasgow to London mail train described how he grappled on the footplate with the masked gang who ambushed his train. The raid, he said, went 'like a military operation'.

**Monday 12**   **"Police Protection for Mail Trains"** Until further notice, unarmed railway police will be on board the nightly travelling Post Offices and the police surveillance at the few stations where they stop is to be intensified.

## HERE IN BRITAIN

### "Queen Opens Power Station"

Blaenau Ffestiniog, a slate quarry town with a population of 7,000, has always been notorious for its heavy rainfall and it was water in unlimited quantities that brought them prosperity in the form of a pumped storage hydro- electric scheme six years ago.

Heavy clouds hung over the town just before the Queen arrived to open the £15m pumped storage power station, but the sun broke through to help the 500 guests welcome her. Declaring the world's largest pumped storage power station open, the Queen said, *"Electric power is becoming more and more important, as we found out last winter."*

## AROUND THE WORLD

### "Unofficial Record in Three-Wheeler"

A jet engined, three-wheel car driven by American Craig Breedlove of Los Angeles, set up a new unofficial world land speed record on the Bonneville salt flats in Utah. The average speed attained by 'The Spirit of America' for two runs along the flats was 408 mph.

Under present international rules for world land speed records, John Cobb's 16-year-old record of 394.196 mph will continue to stand as 'The Spirit of America' is jet powered and has only three wheels whereas the rules state it must have at least four wheels and be propelled by at least two of the wheels.

A major earthquake in a populous region like that experienced in Yugoslavia last week, is such a disaster that we tend to forget that the number of earth tremors is some millions a year. Those which cause significant damage, number a little less than a thousand a year. The qualification is 'intensity' of disturbance at any point on the land area of the earth, not necessarily populous. For about 400 earthquakes a year, more than one a day, there is enough information about their origin to provide data and about three a year, release an amount of energy within a factor of six of the greatest recorded in modern times. This is a different criterion from 'intensity' and is expressed approximately as the 'magnitude'.

Most earthquakes originate at depths not greater than 20 miles and are caused, in general, by the relief of stresses which are a legacy from the last great period of mountain-building, and the main lines of their distribution are widely known. In the biggest, the energy release is the same as that in bigger thermonuclear explosions, but because they are the 'endpoint' of a series of much smaller events, they are very difficult to predict.

Most progress in deduction has been in using the waves from major earthquakes to understand the interior structure of the earth and much less in understanding the processes involved in the build-up of stresses and their eventual, sudden relief. There are far too many earth tremors for 'warning tremors' to be useful. In a few cases, notably the famous San Andreas fault in California, and New Zealand, whose movements have been under continuous observation for many years, it may be possible to say that a stage of danger has been reached. To set a date, or even a year, for the moment of release is another question.

# IN THE NEWS

**Tuesday 13**    **"16 Dead After Airliner Hits Farmhouse"** 16 passengers and crew on board a Viscount airliner were killed when it crashed on a farmhouse during a thunderstorm about 15 miles north of Lyons.

**Wednesday 14**    **"Robbers Farmhouse Hideout"** A lonely Oxfordshire farmhouse was the hideout for the train robbers. Mailbags and an Army type truck and two Land-Rovers have been found but no money.

**Thursday 15**    **"French Troops on Guard"** French tanks and parachute troops, at the request of the President, are helping police and gendarmerie restore order in Brazzaville, capital of the Republic of the Congo, where a state of siege was declared.

**Friday 16**    **"New National Paper"** Plans are in train by IPC who control the Mirror group, to replace the Daily Herald with a completely new daily newspaper which would be still a newspaper of the left but would be completely independent.

**Saturday 17**    **"Lost Leonardo Claimed"** American art experts claim to have discovered a painting by Leonardo da Vinci considered lost for about 400 years. The painting, 'Christ among the Doctors', is on show at an art gallery in New York.

**Sunday 18**    **"What a Busman's Holiday"** The bus drivers and other transport workers with families and friends were looking forward to their day-at-the-seaside in Margate – but their bus only managed two miles through London before getting stuck under a railway bridge!

**Monday 19**    **"Britain's Biggest Strike for 6 Years"** On nearly 500 building sites chosen by union leaders, 150,000 workers held a week's 'guerrilla' strike for more pay and a 40hr week.

## HERE IN BRITAIN
### "All For the Want of an Archaeologist"

The search for treasure thought to be worth £3m lying 10ft under a ruined chapel at Basing House, Basingstoke, is being held up by the lack of a qualified, Ministry approved, archaeologist to supervise the digging.

The gold is reputed to have been buried in 1645 by the owner's ancestor, the Marquess of Winchester, during the siege of Basing House when 300 Royalists held out against Cromwell for three years. Dozens of volunteers are eager to help in recovering the fortune, understood to be in the form of a solid gold table and 6-ton statue of a calf.

## AROUND THE WORLD
### "Troops to Descend on Pallets"

Landing troops in the battle area without using parachutes is being tried out by the US Air Force. The soldiers will sit in 'people pallets' which will be dropped from low-flying assault aircraft. The pallets, which hold up to 48 men, sit on the open cargo ramp at the rear of the aircraft which will fly over the delivery area at up to 35ft between 115 and 159mph.

A trailing hook on the pallet engages a steel cable on the ground, the pallet is pulled off and falls, sliding 100ft and stopping gradually. The shock? *'Less than that when riding in a fast lift'.*

# BIGGER SHIPS IN LONDON

PORT OF LONDON AUTHORITY

By providing radio commentary of tidal information to ships' masters and pilots, the Port of London Authority hope to make the Thames safely navigable to ships some 10,000 tons bigger than the present size limit. They hope to do this cheaply, without further dredging, and the scheme needs Government permission to cover an area extending some 22 miles to the east of their present boundary at the Nore.

The PLA believe they have found on the 'Shivering Sand', a shallow, sand bar in the Thames estuary nine miles north of Herne Bay, an answer to their navigation problem. Anti-aircraft gun forts built during the war to defend London still stand on the 'Shivering Sand' above high-water level. The PLA would like to attach to one of the forts a tide-gauging apparatus. The machine would continuously register the height of the tide and radio the information to a shore station. It would be unmanned and need servicing only occasionally. The continuous tidal information measured directly from this point in the centre of the estuary would be immeasurably more valuable to navigators than the tidal prediction tables used at present.

Such accurate knowledge of tidal conditions would enable ships of 43ft draught, 4ft greater than the present maximum, to enter the Port of London when the tides were right which would mean ships of some 65,000 tons gross, perhaps by the middle of 1965. The largest ship ever to have entered the port up to now is a loaded tanker of 55,000 tons gross. Last year the Port of London maintained its dominance of British trade, handling 32.6% of the nation's trade by value. The net registered tonnage arriving in and departing the Port was more than 94m tons - the highest figure ever recorded.

# IN THE NEWS

**Tuesday 20**    **"Building Strike Halts Major Projects"** Hundreds of sites were closed including the Tilbury power station, the Trawsfynydd nuclear power station site and cathedrals on Merseyside.

**Wednesday 21**    **"Bus Stop' Jet is a Winner"** Britain's BAC One-Eleven made a triumphant, 28-minute, maiden flight. Two years ahead of its nearest rival in short haul passenger flying, it has won orders in excess of £50m without even taking off.

**Thursday 22**    **"Guns Against Monks"** In South Vietnam, martial law was imposed by the Catholic President and troops arrested hundreds of Buddhist monks and nuns as the religious dispute flared into an international crisis.

**Friday 23**    **"Duncan Sandys Flies to Malaya Crisis"** The Minister hopes to avoid a crisis by supporting the Premier of Malaya against Indonesia's opposition to the new Malaysian Federation, a merging of Malaya, Singapore, North Borneo and Sarawak.

**Saturday 24**    **"Clydebank to Build £7m Liner"** John Brown and Co are to build a passenger liner for the Swedish American Line. The gross tonnage will be over 24,000 tons and the ship will be designed especially with cruising in mind.

**Sunday 25**    **"Emigration to Canada Rises Sharply"** Figures released by the British immigration department show that 41,444 settlers arrived in Canada between January and June compared with 34,061 in the corresponding period last year.

**Monday 26**    **"Soviet Trawler Hides Radar Equipment"** New equipment observed on Russian trawlers, already over-loaded with electronic devices, by British and American warships in the Bay of Biscay suggest that it could jam the radar of NATO navies.

## HERE IN BRITAIN

### ""Roman Coin Proves It"

The remains of a wooden ship found embedded in mud near Blackfriars Bridge, were identified 'without a doubt' as Roman when a small bronze coin was found in the mast step.

The coin, still bright, bears the raised head of Domitian who was Roman emperor from AD 81 to 96, and who was murdered by a freedman, stands out clearly. It was an old tradition that when a mast was stepped - placed in position - a coin was placed under its heel. It is thought that it was intended to be an offering to the gods for good winds.

## AROUND THE WORLD

### "Floodlit Golfing"

A golf club in New Jersey has installed floodlights over a nine-hole course and will be opening for night play to satisfy the desire of Americans to play golf at any time of the day or night.

There are not enough courses to meet the demand of the five and a half million golfers. Fairways have become as congested as the highways leading in and out of the major cities. The lights should be adequate for the fairways and greens but those who consistently stray from the recommended route from tee to green are advised to carry a torch.

# ROULETTE ALL AT SEA

A British liner will be putting to sea this winter with a roulette table on board. Royal Mail Lines are to install the table in the cruise liner 'Andes' as an experiment. Special chips are being made and stakes will range from 2s 6d (12p) to about £100. Crockfords will provide trained croupiers from Le Touquet and the table will first be used when the Andes sails on a 16-day Christmas cruise from Southampton. Later roulette will be available during a 64-day winter cruise to India and the Far East.

Shipboard gambling has evolved in three mild forms in passenger liners. Nearly all ships provide bingo, horse racing in which the purser throws dice and model horses are moved down a table-top course, and the 'totalisator' which is a sweepstake on the daily run made good by the ship. Other shipping companies will be observing the progress with interest. It is far from certain whether there is a demand for harder gambling at sea. Cunard found evidence to the contrary. Fruit machines were installed in the Queen Mary and the Queen Elizabeth some two years ago, but they were removed after two trips. *"A lot of passengers objected"*.

The history of roulette began in 17th century France with a mathematician named Blaise Pascal who was in search of a perpetual motion machine for an experiment that he was conducting involving a wheel much like the modern-day roulette one. The wheels current form is a combination of the English wheel games, Italian board games and a French board game named roulette. In 1843, two French brothers, Francois and Louis Blanc, founded the first casinos in Monte Carlo and altered the wheel, revolutionising the game of roulette. Legend has it that they sold their souls to the Devil in exchange for these ideas... and the secret to roulette!

# AUG 27TH - SEPT 2ND 1963

## IN THE NEWS

**Tuesday 27**     **"Ready for Rescue"** Rescue workers at a coal-mine in Pennsylvania completed the drilling of an escape shaft to a narrow chamber 308ft below ground in which two men have been trapped for the past 13 days.

**Wednesday 28**    **"41 Hour Week for Builders"** The dispute in the building industry settled with the unions accepting new offers on wages and hours spread over the next three years. 200,000 men have been on strike.

**Thursday 29**     **"Washington's Disciplined Protest"** President Kennedy called on the American people to *'accelerate our effort to achieve equal rights for all our citizens'*. His Labour Day plea was released early to coincide with the civil rights demonstration.

**Friday 30**     **"General De Gaulle's Help"** Implying criticism of American policies, the French President made a personal offer of *'cordial cooperation'* by France in any national effort that the Vietnamese might undertake to surmount their crisis.

**Saturday 31**     **"Go-Ahead for the TSR 2"** A Ministry of Aviation statement said, *"In addition to the orders already placed for the TSR 2 for development and introductory flying by the RAF, BAC have been authorised to enable production of TSR 2s for squadron service to begin."*

**Sunday Sept 1**    **"Future States of Malaysia Celebrate"** Complete independence for the state of Singapore and self-government for the colonies of North Borneo and Sarawak were proclaimed in Malaya. The four will form Malaysia.

**Monday 2**     **"Stranded Britons"** Riot police were called in to keep order at Calais when angry British tourists hammered at quayside gates to get on board ferries to England. The trouble began when motorists without reservations were given places when they just 'turned up'.

---

### HERE IN BRITAIN

#### "Joyful Pitch Invasion"

The West Indies beat England by eight wickets in the fifth Test match at the Oval, thereby winning the series and sparking scenes as are seldom witnessed on an English ground. Every West Indian in the crowd of 25,000, flooded onto the field. Earlier they had encroached on the boundary ropes, the West Indians bursting with enthusiasm and joy.

In the rush that followed, Hunte was *'as a swimmer being dumped by the waves.'* He made the safety of the pavilion, having lost his bat on the way. Four stumps and two bails were also surrendered in the charge.

---

### AROUND THE WORLD

#### "Two Weeks Ordeal Underground"

Two of the three miners trapped more than 300 feet below ground for two weeks in Pennsylvania, were hauled from the earth alive. Wearing a parachute harness, greased overalls and football helmets they were lifted to the surface by a winch manned by rescue workers who had been struggling to free them from their deep prison since their position was first discovered a week ago. After the initial jubilation at being rescued, both men became preoccupied with the fate of their colleague. Drilling then began on a new escape shaft to the area where they believed he could be lying.

# MARTIN LUTHER KING

Vice President Lyndon B. Johnson and Attorney General Robert F. Kennedy with King, Benjamin Mays, and other civil rights leaders, June 22, 1963

King gave his most famous speech, "I Have a Dream", before the Lincoln Memorial during the 1963 March on Washington for Jobs and Freedom.June 22, 1963

The largest Negro demonstration for freedom since the abolition of slavery took place in Washington, peacefully. More than 200,000 came in a vast but orderly throng to the Lincoln Memorial to demand freedom now. They had come a long way since the first freedom buses were burnt by white mobs and southern policemen had turned dogs and fire hoses on them. All wore badges showing clasped black and white hands and some carried banners with the legend "Freedom in '63". Just before noon they began to march slowly down Constitution and Independence Avenues to the Lincoln Memorial. They marched about 20 abreast, to the music of brass bands, many singing "John Brown's Body" and holding picket signs with demands for freedom, jobs, housing and schools.

At the memorial, the Rev. Martin Luther King, addressed them. *"Five score years ago the great American in whose shadow we stand today signed the emancipation proclamation. . . . One hundred years later the Negro is still crippled by the manacles of segregation and the chains of discrimination. I have a dream that my four little children will one day live in a nation where they will not be judged by the colour of their skin but by the content of their character.*

*I have a dream that one day every valley shall be engulfed, every hill shall be exalted and every mountain shall be made low, the rough places will be made plains and the crooked places will be made straight and the glory of the Lord shall be revealed and all flesh shall see it together. Go back to Mississippi. Go back to Alabama. Go back to Georgia, to Louisiana, and the northern slums. Go back knowing that all this will end one day. We will hew hope out of the mountain of despair. Let freedom ring."*

# SEPT 3RD - 9TH 1963

## IN THE NEWS

**Tuesday 3**    **"Bachelor Ban"** As a result of a Government ruling in the wake of the Vassall spy case, selection for the post of service attaches to embassies in certain foreign capitals will be restricted to married men on the grounds that bachelors are believed to be especially vulnerable to blackmail by enemy agents.

**Wednesday 4**    **"Daily Herald Reprieved"** As the result of a direct request from Harold Wilson, Leader of the Labour Party, plans to supersede the Herald with a new national, radical, daily, will be postponed until after the General Election.

**Thursday 5**    **"Alabama Schools Closed"** The day-old attempt to desegregate three schools in Birmingham, came to an end after a night of rioting in which one Negro was killed and the house of a Negro lawyer bombed.

**Friday 6**    **"Christine Keeler Arrested"** The "missing model" now embroiled in the Profumo affair was charged with conspiracy to obstruct the course of justice, with perjury.

**Saturday 7**    **"Wilson Fights Gag on Denning"** Leaders of the Labour Party are determined to ensure that newspaper reports of Lord Denning's inquiry into the Profumo affair will not be gagged by the threat of libel actions.

**Sunday 8**    **"Jim Clark Wins World Championship"** After a thrilling duel with John Surtees and Graham Hill, the Scottish driver won the Italian Grand Prix to become World Champion.

**Monday 9**    **"Last Voyage of The Medway Queen"** The last Thames paddle steamer crossed from Herne Bay to Southend on her final day of service. Her future is still in doubt but there are hopes for her preservation.

## HERE IN BRITAIN

### "Depth Charges off Brixham"

Six live depth-charges were lost by a ship of the Royal Navy taking part in 'Exercise Union' off the south Devon coast. They did not explode when they were dropped, and their exact position is not known, but it was in an area used by the inshore fishing fleet eight miles off Brixham.

They are lying at a depth of 27 fathoms, on the sea-bed and could be trawled up by a fishing boat and might explode. The fishery protection vessel 'Watchful' stood by and all shipping was warned of the hazards, but *"there was no danger to normal shipping"*.

## AROUND THE WORLD

### "Not Gold Enough"

About 1,000 goldsmiths demonstrated before the Indian Parliament building demanding the withdrawal of the Government's gold control order, which bans the manufacture and sale of pure gold ornaments. Thousands of goldsmiths have been thrown out of work as a result of the order which restricts the manufacture of ornaments to 14-carat gold. There has been a virtual standstill in demand for 14-carat gold trinkets from a public long accustomed to using pure gold ornaments. The order was intended to stop smuggling and unearth hoarded gold to be used for purchases from abroad. It has so far not been a complete success!

# THE MEDWAY QUEEN

With a blast on her siren, the paddle steamer Medway Queen heaved away from the pier at Herne Bay, on the Kent bank of the Thames, for the last time this month, watched by the Mayoress and a small crowd of well-wishers. Among the 500 passengers for the final voyage were a considerable number of "regulars", one of them, a chauffeur from Highgate, has enjoyed the trip two or three times each year for the last 20 years. Medway Queen steamed at 12 knots towards Southend pier for another ceremonial farewell before returning to Strood pier near Rochester

The 316-ton steamer has plied the Thames estuary since she was built on the Clyde in 1923 and entered service on the Strood-Chatham-Southend-Herne Bay route the following year. With occasional excursions elsewhere she served on the same route until the beginning of the Second World War when she was requisitioned for the Royal Navy and converted for mine sweeping.

In 1940 HMS Medway Queen joined the 10th Mine-sweeping Flotilla based in Dover where, in May-June 1940, she played a key part in 'Operation Dynamo'. Medway Queen and her crew made seven return trips across the channel to bring the men home from Dunkirk. The ship's crew estimated that they evacuated 7,000 men while shooting down three Axis aircraft. She remained an active minesweeper until late 1943 after which she was eventually refitted and returned to civilian use with the famous Invicta motif on her funnel. In 1953, Medway Queen was included in the Coronation Naval Review at Spithead.

Her owners said that the Medway Queen's future was still in doubt, but the Paddle Steamer Preservation Society is considering launching an appeal to save the ship from being broken up.

# SEPT 10TH-16TH 1963

## IN THE NEWS

**Tuesday 10**    **"Order Served on Governor"** A court order was served on George Wallace, Governor of Alabama, to cease interfering with the entry of Negro pupils to schools in Birmingham, Mobile and Tuskegee.

**Wednesday 11** **"Two New Power Stations"** Two more new power stations are to be built, bigger than any in service at present, at Fiddler's Ferry near Warrington and Cottam in Nottinghamshire. They will burn some 9m tons of coal a year and cost about £150m.

**Thursday 12**    **"Smashing 'Harvest' of Fruit"** A train derailed in Kent shedding thousands of pounds' worth of grapes, peaches, apples and pears. Of 29 wagons, 24 carried fruit and 19 of those came off the line.

**Friday 13**    **"36 British Tourists Die in Pyrenees Air Crash"** The French Viking flying from Gatwick to Perpignan, was swept off course by a violent storm and crashed in the mountains.

**Saturday 14**    **"Police Book the Festival Nude"** A young model at the Edinburgh Festival has been charged that she *"did act in a shameless and indecent manner … in full view of those present allow herself to be wheeled nude across the gallery on a trolley"*.

**Sunday 15**    **"Four Children Killed by Bomb in Negro Church"** The explosion came six days after the city of Birmingham had desegregated four public schools despite the objections of the Governor, George Wallace.

**Monday 16**    **"Top Scientists Turn to US for Jobs"** The Government's failure to plan at Aldermaston for alternative civilian work to be done by scientists influences young scientists in deciding whether to take jobs in a defence establishment or to seek careers abroad."

### HERE IN BRITAIN
#### "Bank Notes Whiter Than White"

Five-pound notes are blue, one-pound notes green and 10s notes brown, but after they have been in a washing machine with a detergent they come out as a perfectly white sheet.

An article on mutilated notes in 'The Bank of England Bulletin' states, *"Washing machines are the most common source of damage. Others include the appetites of dogs, other pets and even small children; fire and water; rotted notes which have been buried in the garden or hidden under floorboards. Attempts to foil the burglar by hiding notes in the stove or up the chimney, lead to many disasters when fires are lit later."*

### AROUND THE WORLD
#### "Comedy of Errors"

The Grand Theatre Geneva was reopened with a ceremonial flourish last December, 11 years after it had been severely damaged by fire, *'at all costs'* before the new installations were functioning properly.

The fire alarm which automatically brings five fire engines racing to the spot has so far gone off accidentally 10 times, the air conditioning system sometimes introduces cooking smells into the auditorium or emits freezing cold air, lifts are erratic, scene shifting mechanisms faulty and what is more, occupants of the first five or six rows of seats in the stalls cannot see the ballet dancers' feet.

# THE BUMBLEBEE FARM

Bumblebees are being bred in captivity in a Cardiff college to help prepare for a possible shortage. The precaution is being taken because of the number of bumblebees being killed by crop-spraying and weed-killers and there is a danger that numbers will be reduced such that agriculture will be affected.

The bumblebee is essential to the production of the seed of red clover which is one of the main cattle foods. No other bee has a tongue long enough to reach into the flower tube of the clover and bring out the nectar on which, together with pollen, larvae feed. The honeybee will visit red clover only if it needs pollen, in which case it, too, will pollinate the crop, but this does not usually occur until towards the end of the season, when the main flowering of the red clover is over.

This month, queen bumblebees have been laid to rest for the winter in separate small boxes placed in a refrigerator. They are the first few dozen of the 200 to 300 for whom a safe hibernation is hoped. The bees were caught in local gardens and hedgerows. In greenhouses, where the queens are mated with males, they are provided with paper artificial flowers which have tubes filled with sugar solution, the bees' staple diet, attached.

While the males die after mating, the queens go on to hibernate and in the following year produce the next generation of worker males and queens. If queens can be persuaded to start nests in spring in specially constructed boxes, when the colony has gathered strength, they might be taken to the clover fields suffering from a shortage of bees - rather like gangs of construction workers brought on to sites. There is an alternative, the breeding of a variety of red clover with a flower tube short enough for an ordinary honeybee.

## IN THE NEWS

**Tuesday 17**   **"Mr Kennedy's Deep Sense of Outrage"** Altogether 1,400 National Guardsmen, state troopers and policemen stood guard after a night of rioting. FBI agents continued their search for the perpetrators of the church explosion that killed four young Negro girls.

**Wednesday 18** **"New Year Baby"** It was announced from Balmoral where she is spending a family holiday, that the Queen is expecting her fourth baby in the new year.

**Thursday 19**  **"Mob Attacks British Embassy"** Thousands of demonstrators stormed the British Embassy in Jakarta brandishing slogans denouncing the new Federation of Malaysia.

**Friday 20**    **"Police Severely Tested by Rise in Crime"** Criminal Statistics show that the biggest increases in crime was for breaking and entering, receiving, frauds and false pretences and larceny. Only a small increase in the crimes of violence was recorded.

**Saturday 21**  **"Seabed Drilling for Oil Starts"** The British Petroleum Company is gambling that oil is beneath the sea off Lulworth Cove. There are good reasons for their optimism, the largest oil well in Britain is already in production at Kimmeridge, only a few miles away.

**Sunday 22**    **"Let's Go to the Moon Together"** President Kennedy suggested America and Russia should send a joint expedition to the moon "someday this decade". It came as a surprise as he had 'cold shouldered' the same suggestion from Mr K last year.

**Monday 23**    **"British Liner Trapped on Reef"** The luxury cruise liner 'Andes', carrying 450 cocktail-sipping passengers on a Mediterranean cruise, ran aground off Sicily, but was re-floated, undamaged after three hours.

## HERE IN BRITAIN

### "Easier to Win a Million"

The fixed odds 'pools war' heated up this week when William Hill announced "New 'all-time record' odds of 250,000 to 1. All you do is correctly forecast five aways and five draws."

When chief rivals Ladbroke's heard, they retaliated, "We will give odds of one million to one – all you do is forecast six correct scores." Hills then replied they had already been offering minimum odds of 1m and maximum of 24m, for six correct scores. One month they paid £43,392 for 2d (1p) stakes, the winning odds - 3,960,000 to 1. Ladbroke's said, "Their list only offers 10 matches to choose from, ours covers 55!"

## AROUND THE WORLD

### "France May End Tourist Petrol"

There were reports in Paris that foreign motorists in France will no longer be issued with petrol coupons at a cheaper price than domestic consumers pay. If tourist coupons are abolished, it will cause great disappointment among British holidaymakers, both those travelling in France and the, many more, who regularly cross France to Spain, Switzerland and Italy.

These coupons represent a worthwhile saving on the higher cost of most grades of petrol. Premium grades vary between 6s 5d (32p) and 6s 9d a gallon, but with the coupons British tourists can buy the same for 5s 5d (27p), only a little more than the 4s 9d (24p) here at home.

# CONTROLLING PEDESTRIANS

*The first experiment was in Harringay, London and opened by the Transport Minister, Mr Marples.*

Rules for Britain's first pedestrian control experiment have been published. The scheme is designed to give pedestrians complete protection at certain crossing points in return for giving up their right to cross the road anywhere else. The penalty for crossing at an unauthorised place will be a fine of up to £20 and the experiment, which will last 12 months, will begin in three places in London. Three sites - each about half a mile long – will be designated as 'pedestrian control areas, their boundaries marked by painted red lines and signs erected with crossings about 100 yards apart.

A pedestrian will find himself faced by a signal on the opposite side of the road showing either 'Do not cross' or 'Cross' with a symbol of a pedestrian between them. When he presses a button a blue light will appear on a panel beside the pedestrian, and the 'Do not cross' sign in red will appear on the signal. When this is replaced by the 'Cross' sign the pedestrian symbol will begin to move, and pedestrians should then cross. After six seconds the 'Cross' signal will change back and after that no more pedestrians must step off the kerb and the pedestrian figure will begin a rapid walking movement as a warning that the crossing period is nearly over. Motorists will be warned when a crossing is in use by red 'Stop' signals.

Outside the hours of the experiment, it will not be illegal for pedestrians to cross the road at places other than the controlled crossings and drivers must expect to find this, and the new experiment should not be confused with panda crossings, which were designed only to assist pedestrians in difficult traffic conditions. Although the push-button method of operation is similar, the public would not find the new experiment as complicated as the panda one!

# SEPT 24TH-30TH 1963

## IN THE NEWS

**Tuesday 24**     **"Clash Over Decimal Currency"** A government report has caused controversy. Businesses favour a system based on a major unit worth 10s. The City advocate retention of the pound sterling because of the 'international goodwill' it carries.

**Wednesday 25**     **"Lord Denning's Verdict"** His report on the Profumo affair, criticising the PM and Ministers, sold 4,000 copies in the first hour when it went on sale at half past midnight.

**Thursday 26**     **"No More 'Guilty but Insane'"** A Criminal Law Revision report proposes the change to 'Not guilty by reason of insanity'. The present form of verdict is regarded by lawyers as an anomaly; it is an acquittal.

**Friday 27**     **"Denning Report – Pressure on Macmillan"** There will be no early general election, but Harold Macmillan is expected to retire soon.

**Saturday 28**     **"Mass Escape from Broadmoor Foiled"** Police foiled a fantastic plot to murder a guard and set free 20 mental patients. Three books had been delivered in the post, each with a hacksaw concealed in their spines.

**Sunday 29**     **"BOAC Plane in Landing Drama"** The nose wheel of one of its Boeing 707 airliners collapsed on landing at Idlewild airport, New York. The plane with 66 passengers and 10 crew had turned back to New York after a fire warning light came on.

**Monday 30**     **"Fears Rise for Safety"** The British consul in Jakarta, called for the 'immediate evacuation' of 140 British women and children from the Shell oil plant at Balikpapan, in east Indonesian Borneo. The town is under the command of bitterly anti-British forces.

## HERE IN BRITAIN

### "Frozen But Not Cold"

New techniques for preserving food are being developed in Aberdeen by Unilever, in order to provide a better quality and a greater variety of prepacked meals. Food producers were given an opportunity to see the latest accelerated freeze-drying equipment, which does remarkable things to the most commonplace meats and vegetables.

Once the dried product is placed in water for use, it rapidly assumes its original form. Market research of certain meals compared to conventional air-dried foods is being carried out and if public reaction is favourable the production of freeze-dried foods on a commercial scale in Britain will start next year.

## AROUND THE WORLD

### "Mafia Kiss of Death"

Television viewers in the US witnessed the telling of a real-life drama of crime and violence that made the usual fare served up by the network seem almost suitable for children's hour.

Joseph Valachi, a self-confessed murderer condemned to death by the Cosa Nostra, described by the Attorney General as a private government of organised crime, told the Senate and banks of television cameras of more than 30 years of murder and crime under the protection of the syndicate.

A squat, elderly man, with dyed red hair, he spoke in gutter Brooklynese and appeared occasionally a little impatient with the committee for not understanding!

# TREADING THE GRAPES

The Quinta de la Rosa is one of many farms scattered all over the steep slopes of the terraced vineyards in the Alto Douro valley. At the end of September, peasants come swarming in with their women and children from neighbouring hills or from across the Spanish border to pick the grapes. All day long until sundown you hear the music that accompanies the procession of basket carriers from and to near and distant vineyards, and as they approach the house to tip their 130lb loads into the huge rectangular granite vats, or lagares, that are built on the basement floor of the adega. The grapes are carefully picked, only the sound ones are thrown into the lagar with their stems and all.

At dusk the vats are filled, and the men climb in to tread the fruit (having carefully washed their feet beforehand). Their gaily coloured pants rolled up, the men go tramping up and down in line across the lagar, first moving the heavy mass of clusters with wooden poles, then continuing with their arms linked, lifting their red and purple legs in a 'high knee action' to the rhythm of a drummer, an accordion player and their singing while their wives, village neighbours and children of all ages make this an occasion for a merry-go-round on the floor of the adega until the early hours of the morning.

Although there are now a number of mechanised wine making adegas in the Douro, the old traditional method of production is likely to continue in this quinta for some years to come, and it still remains an open question whether mechanisation can get quite as much colour out of the skins or vie with the firm, yielding touch of the human foot which crushes the grapes to liquid.

# IN THE NEWS

**Tuesday 1**    **"Britain to Join Talks on Nuclear Force"** Britain is to take part in discussions to be held in Paris and Washington, on the establishment of a multilateral nuclear force for the North Atlantic Treaty Organisation.

**Wednesday 2**    **"The Sally Army Has a New General"** The Salvation Army has elected Commissioner Frederick Coutts who has spent the last six years in Australia. The new leader will need to keep the Army in step with the changing pattern of the world.

**Thursday 3**    **"Jumping Jet Crashes"** Britain's revolutionary SC-1 vertical take-off jet plunged to the ground 20ft above Short's airfield in Belfast during a test flight. The pilot was killed.

**Friday 4**    **"Britain's Demoralised Doctors"** A report on the demoralisation of family doctors stated, *"The present method of remuneration offers scant encouragement to good doctoring, since the heavy expenses required for a high standard of premises, staffing, equipment and organisation have to be met from the doctor's gross income".*

**Saturday 5**    **"Big Drop in Inflow of Migrants"** The flow of Commonwealth immigrants into Britain was cut by about three-quarters during the first 12 months of the working of the Commonwealth Immigrants Act, 1962. The biggest reduction being from the West Indies.

**Sunday 6**    **"Police Appeal to 'Find Buster'"** Scotland Yard believe Ronald 'Buster' Edwards wanted in connection with the Great Train Robbery is back from his trip to the Continent.

**Monday 7**    **"Dr Beeching to Pare Trunk Lines"** Plans for the second stage of the reshaping of British Railways, involving the rationalisation of trunk services and the elimination of some main lines, are receiving finishing touches.

## HERE IN BRITAIN

### "Marples Matchstick Men"

The Minister of Transport's little blue matchstick men came into being this week at the three selected London sites and, despite the somewhat complicated procedure which now must become second nature to all pedestrians who wish to cross the selected roads, no casualties were reported on the first day.

However, Mr Marples was performing the opening ceremonies and experienced one of the hazards of even the best of regulated crossings when a woman on a bicycle ignored both the red lights and the matchstick men and narrowly escaped making history 'by knocking down the Minister'.

## AROUND THE WORLD

### "Deadly Hurricane Flora"

More than 6,000 people were killed by Hurricane Flora as it rampaged through the Caribbean in the past two weeks. The WHO has estimated that 5,000 died in Haiti and more than 1,000 when the hurricane battered the eastern end of Cuba for five successive days. Thousands of homes, roads and railways were destroyed and crops and cattle obliterated. Thousands of peasant families and agricultural workers lost everything they possessed. The toll of destruction and death places it on record as the deadliest storm ever to have emerged in the tropical Atlantic surpassing that which hit Galveston, Texas, in 1900, when nearly 6,000 people were killed.

# TREE TRANSPLANT

Instant trees are now available in Britain and could make a huge difference to the face of the country. At Trowell open cast mining site, watchers saw a large digger uproot two trees and transplant them to a site nearby within a matter of minutes. The diggers can uproot trees 60ft high and 16in in diameter. The shovel cuts through the outer roots but preserves the root ball intact, the trees are then picked up by the machine and carried away. Fewer than one in 10 dies after transplantation.

This American process was introduced to Britain in the past two weeks by Scottish Land Development acting with the National Coal Board. The spokesman suggested the technique would be developed in many ways. *"Hundreds of thousands of trees are killed in this country every year,"* he said, *"we are now in touch with the Ministry of Transport, who must move 400,000 trees in the next five years. The prospects are limitless."*

Each tree costs only a few pounds to move and those which have to be moved from a building site could be assembled in tree banks. Transplantation would preserve grown trees as well as providing a quick screen. It could also, for instance, help local authorities worried about damage to young trees on housing estates as trees from a 'doomed wood' could be used.

Opencast mining sites restored in the past had only fences in between the fields which meant that farmers were not given the windbreaks they needed. Now fences and trees could be transplanted to another part of the site as work was going on. *"This is one of the greatest moves forward in this field that has ever been made,"* Lord Robens of the Coal Board said, *"Now the means to hide the ugly scars of coal mining are at our disposal."*

# OCT 8TH - 14TH 1963

## IN THE NEWS

**Tuesday 8**  "Haiti Death Roll Over 2,000" For the past four days Hurricane Flora has raged over Cuba and latest reports from that island indicate that more than half the crops have been destroyed, and many farms and buildings razed.

**Wednesday 9**  "Mr Macmillan to Have Operation" Mr. Macmillan was admitted to hospital on the eve of the Conservative Party Conference, for an operation for prostatic obstruction. It is expected that this will involve his absence from official duties for some weeks.

**Thursday 10**  "First President of Uganda" The Kabaka of Buganda was sworn in amid national rejoicing on the first anniversary of the country's independence from Britain. The Kabaka will exercise the same powers as those of Britain's Governor-General of Uganda.

**Friday 11**  "Mr Macmillan Decides to Resign Soon" After a successful operation in hospital, Mr Macmillan made the surprise announcement that he will step down.

**Saturday 12**  "Algeria Facing Civil War Again" Civil war returned to Algeria barely a year after the end of the bloody seven-year conflict with France. Government troops opened fire on Berber rebels who returned their fire.

**Sunday 13**  "Curb on Opening Car Doors" To open the door of a vehicle in 'such a manner as to cause injury or danger' is now against the law. Before, it was only an offence 'to open the door of a vehicle so as to obstruct the highway'

**Monday 14**  "Cabinet Move to Make Lord Home PM" The choice is now between four candidates: Lord Home, Lord Hailsham, Mr Butler and Mr Maudling and a decision is to be expected this week.

## HERE IN BRITAIN
### "The Bogus Vicar"

A married man, aged 32 with four children, arranged a bogus wedding ceremony at a quiet country church, with his friend posing as a clergyman, to 'bring some happiness' to his girlfriend who was expecting a baby. He hired a cassock from a theatrical costumier and his friend changed into this behind a hedge near the church. He wore a 'dog-collar' but no surplice and conducted the service in the Parish church at Oldberrow, Warwickshire.

Some of the family at the church became suspicious because the register was an ordinary exercise book with the bride and bridegroom's names entered in ink in capital letters.

## AROUND THE WORLD
### "Dam Disaster in Italy"

A vast flood of water from the Vaiont dam, the third highest concrete dam in the world, swept down the Piave valley pouring into several communities in its path. Five villages in the Belluno area of northern Italy were devastated when a landslide from the Toc peak (6,000ft), which overlooks the dam, brought down a huge amount of earth and mud which, mixed with rocks and uprooted trees, caused a gigantic wave that overflowed the dam.

Longarone, a community of 2,000 people close to the dam, was reported to have been 'completely submerged' and the total death toll was estimated at over 3,000.

# A TASTE FOR WHALE MEAT

Whale meat on sale in Tokyo, Japan

Japan's whaling fleets set out this month for the Antarctic with the prospect of seven months at sea before they return home. The whaling companies are sending more ships than ever, and they prosper while the whaling fleets of Europe decline. Japanese fleets now take nearly half of the world's whale catch and it seems likely that within a few years their only remaining rival will be the Soviet Union. The rise of the Japanese whaling fleets has been rapid. Ten years ago, Japan had only two fleets; Norway had nine and Britain three. Today Japan has 10 fleets, of which seven operate in the Antarctic and three in the North Pacific.

As other countries have found whaling less and less profitable, Japan has eagerly bought up their rights and their equipment. In the past year or so she has bought whaling rights from Norway and Britain and recently a Japanese buyer acquired the Southern Harvester, a 15- year-old British factory ship. The reason for the success of the Japanese companies is simply that the Japanese like whale meat. While other countries are mainly interested in oil, for the Japanese fleets oil is only a secondary product. Last year the meat at £100 a ton fetched £30 a ton more than the oil.

A typical Japanese whaling fleet now has a factory ship (about 20,000 tons), a tanker (15,000 tons), two or three cold storage ships (each 10,000 tons), four cargo carriers (each 1,500 tons), and anything up to a dozen 'catcher boats' (each 750 tons). *"Whaling is a dirty business"*, but last year five whaling nations finally agreed on a division of the catch. Japan, Russia, Norway, Britain and the Netherlands. Britain and Norway sold some of their share to Japan immediately and Japan bought the remainder of Britain's share in July this year.

# OCT 15TH-21TH 1963

## IN THE NEWS

**Tuesday 15**   **"Moroccan Army 'Invasion of Algeria'"** Algeria claimed that several thousand men, supported by aircraft and tanks, had invaded her territory in the western Sahara to a depth of about 50 miles.

**Wednesday 16**   **"Dentists Will Get Only 1% Increase"** Britain's 10,000 dentists are angry they will not get the 14% pay rise promised by Mr Macmillan seven months ago.

**Thursday 17**   **"Tokyo-London in Record Time"** A US Air Force B-58 Hustler bomber flew non-stop from Tokyo to London in the record time of 8hr 35min. Twice as fast as the previous Tokyo-London record set in 1957 by a British Canberra jet.

**Friday 18**   **"Russians Allow British Convoys Through"** Four British convoys passed through the Babelsberg checkpoint to west Berlin without incident, after previously being held up for nine hours after a Russian demand that they leave their vehicles to be counted.

**Saturday 19**   **"Alec Douglas Home is Prime Minister"** Mr Macmillan formally resigned and appointed *his* choice of successor, Lord Home, ahead of Mr RA 'Rab' Butler and Mr Reginald Maudling.

**Sunday 20**   ***"TW3 Smashes Complaints Record"*** *Saturday's edition of the satirical show produced hundreds of telephone calls. A spokesman said, "'That Was The Week That Was' always provokes criticism and we do not intend to do anything about it."*

**Monday 21**   **"Good Wishes of East and West"** President Kennedy sent a 'warm and friendly' message to Lord Home, 'looking forward to the continuation of the close and friendly cooperation which has bound our countries so closely for so long.'

## HERE IN BRITAIN

### "Saturday Coal"

The NUM agreed that members might volunteer for shifts on any six Saturdays in November and December in response to a request from the Coal Board for a temporary relaxation of rules. The board want to build up reserves of house coal in case the winter is severe.

Saturday working was introduced during the past two winters but only at pits where a high proportion of large coal is produced. This led to resentment at neighbouring collieries not given the same opportunity for overtime and this year the union has insisted that any pit at which the men are ready to work should open.

## AROUND THE WORLD

### "Felix in Space"

A cat named 'Felix' was launched into space aboard a rocket this week and parachuted safely to earth, the French War Ministry announced. The experiment, which took place at a French base in the Sahara was designed to test the effect of space flight on the cat's brain. It was housed in a small container in the nose of the one-stage rocket and released when the rocket reached its highest point.

The statement said that 'a valuable contribution had been made to the knowledge of how a living creature reacted to a space environment' – which, luckily, implies Felix lived to tell the tale.

# BOOMING BRITISH CAR SALES

New car orders worth nearly £100m were received at the London Motor Show on the first morning even *before* 'the official opening ceremony by Lord Hailsham'. There were crowds at every stand at Earls Court where new, 1964 models, were being presented.

In his opening address Lord Hailsham said, *"I would recommend that the customer, whether he is going to buy a political party or an automobile, to look beyond mere styling which makes a car look good, to the true design which is what fits the car for the road. The British car is a fine monument to British engineering, research, development, design and craftsmanship."*

## RECORD SALES REPORTED

ROVER: So many visitors thronged the Rover company's stand to see the new 2 litre saloon that record breaking orders made it the "Star of the Show."

FORD: A total order worth £6.25m from car hire companies alone and orders for the Corsair already totalled £2.5m.

The ROOTES Group reported orders for the Hillman Minx V, Sunbeam Rapier, Husky and Singers, worth £12m plus £10m order for the rear- engine Hillman Imp.

STANDARD-TRIUMPH: Orders for the new Triumph 2000 in Britain reached £8m.

# OCT 22ND - 28TH 1963

## IN THE NEWS

**Tuesday 22** **"I Know How the Other Half Lives"** Lord Home denies he has 'led a sheltered life'. He said, *"I lived among miners for 20 years, I'm a farmer, I know all about farm work."*

**Wednesday 23** **"BAC One-Eleven "Suddenly Dropped"** In the second blow to British aviation this month, seven crew were killed when a 'bus stop' airliner crashed on a test flight.

**Thursday 24** **"28 More UK Universities Needed"** The Government has accepted the revised targets for the expansion of higher education over the next two decades set out in the Robbins report. By 1980-81 there will be about 60 universities compared with 32 today.

**Friday 25** **"Australia to Buy American Bombers"** They are to buy two squadrons of F-111 A aircraft so the TSR 2, the new British tactical strike and reconnaissance aircraft, will not be flying with the Royal Australian Air Force.

**Saturday 26** **"War on Stamps"** Some of Britain's biggest stores made an attack on trading stamp gift schemes. They told the housewife she is not getting something for nothing, in the end she will be the loser.

**Sunday 27** **"Race to Save Three in Flooded Mine"** Rescuers made telephone contact with three survivors in an air pocket 300ft below the surface in the flooded iron ore mine at Lengede, near Brunswick, Germany.

**Monday 28** **"US Likely to Revise Space Plans"** Soviet withdrawal from the race to put a man on the moon, puts the US in a quandary. It was the fear of another Soviet sputnik victory that persuaded President Kennedy to declare a race!

## HERE IN BRITAIN

### "Police Stop 'The Adorable Idiot'"

Brigitte Bardot was stopped from filming, 'The Adorable Idiot' in London because the crowds who fought to see the blonde French star caused too much chaos in Hampstead'. Brigitte will now go back to Paris to film the scenes. She said, *"No more will I think Englishmen are unemotional. This sort of thing has never happened in France."*

Dressed in knee length boots, corduroy tights and a grey sweater she spoke of the problems of being a 'sex symbol'. *"Why do people go mad like this? Well, I admit I have a certain something – I won't say what – but I certainly have it, don't I?"*

## AROUND THE WORLD

### "Bus Children Saved by a 'Mum'"

A Welsh woman saved the lives of 34 British schoolchildren when the driver of their Army school bus slumped dead at the wheel on a busy German motorway. The bus suddenly slowed, then lunged forward. Mrs Andrews, mother of four children on the bus, noticed that the driver had collapsed and ran forward, took hold of the wheel and pulled the handbrake as the bus left the road at 40mph.

She said later, *"I just shut my eyes and was wrestling to stop the bus careering off the Autobahn. I was waiting for the bus behind to come right through us."*

# RESTORING VICTORY

Saving Britain's most famous warship, HMS Victory from decay and restoring her to the condition in which she sailed into battle at Trafalgar has cost more than £300,000 over the past 10 years. Annually £30,000 has gone in repairs and maintenance but this month the Admiralty announced that the first phase of the extensive work which has prevented her from collapsing in the dock at Portsmouth is complete. Work is still going on and defective structures extending round the ship between the completed bottom repairs and those undertaken in the 1920s above the water line need attention. Special purchases of timber have had to be made and, immense pieces of oak and teak have been cut, fashioned, and fitted by craftsmen with tools like those that were used in building the ship at Chatham dockyard in 1759.

Much research has been undertaken to ensure that the cabins in the flagship are as nearly as possible in the same condition as they were at Trafalgar. Nelson's great cabin has been painted in a pastel shade with gold leaf on the beading and pilasters; the curtains are of pure silk. The day cabin is furnished as it was at Trafalgar and the dining cabin, still not completely furnished, will contain a table made from a model constructed at Devonport in about 1800. At the end of the month work will begin on rerigging the ship with Italian hemp. For the work of rerigging, 34 miles of hemp will be required, three tons of spun yarn, 300 yards of old canvas and 224 gallons of tar.

Last year more than 300,000 people visited the Victory and the Save the Victory Fund has contributed £30,000 towards the cost of this and the provision of teak timbers.

To mark the end of the first phase of the work the Board of Admiralty will host a luncheon on board for members of the advisory technical committee, of which Professor Sir Albeit Richardson is chairman.

## IN THE NEWS

**Tuesday 29** "**London Bus Overtime Ban**" The ban due to start tomorrow and London Transport's threats to call of pay talks scheduled for Friday, could mean a long, crippling dispute.

**Wednesday 30** "**Comedian to Stand Against Home**" The 'TW3'star, Willy Rushton is to stand as an independent against Sir Alec Douglas Home in the Kinross & West Perthshire by-election.

**Thursday 31** "**Average Weekly Spend**" A survey of 3,600 people revealed that we spend on average, £17 11s 11d (£17.60) per week on household expenses. It showed a fall in spending on clothes and a rise in that spent on housing.

**Friday Nov 1** "**Mrs Philby has Joined her Husband**" Eleanor Philby, the American wife of Harold 'Kim' Philby, who defected to the Soviet Union last January, has joined her husband in Russia.

**Saturday 2** "**Basic 40-hour Week in the Docks**" Britain's 65,000 dockers agreed by a large majority to accept a conditional offer by the employers to introduce a basic 40-hour week from July 27 next year. There will be an equating increase in time rates but pieceworkers, who make up 55 to 60 % of the labour force, will receive no increase in rates.

**Sunday 3** "**Generals Appoint Buddhist as Premier**" Saigon rejoiced as the religious crisis ended with the coup d'Etat of President Ngo Dinh Diem and his brother.

**Monday 4** "**Drilling Today for 11 More Miners**" Eleven men who were officially declared drowned in the Lengede iron ore mine disaster last week, were found alive today. They are sheltering in a small inlet of a gallery, about 185ft down, above the level of the floodwaters.

## HERE IN BRITAIN

### "You're Under (Arm) Arrest"

Two prisoners escaped from Parkhurst Prison but were quickly recaptured. The police were hot on the trail when a prison officer's car was driven off from his married quarters, crashed nearby and the two occupants ran away. A police constable saw the two men passing and grabbed both. With a man under each arm he went into the road and signalled a passing car. The driver got out to help but the woman passenger screamed and, in the diversion, one of the men slipped away. The police brought in 'Flash', the Island's tracker dog, and within an hour the prisoner had surrendered.

## AROUND THE WORLD

### "The Life and Soul of the Party"

Mr Khrushchev, singing, joking and proposing toast after toast, played the bride's father at the Moscow wedding reception for two of Russia's space pilots, Miss Valentina Tereshkova and Major Andryan Nikolayev. He told the couple, who were married in a 20-minute ceremony, *"If you have a baby there will be no lack of gifts."* At a table where singers were performing for the 300 guests he joined in with a popular modern 'peaceful coexistence' ballad, 'Do the Russians Want War?' The bride, who's own father was killed in the war, sang too, with one arm linked with her 'cosmic father'.

# STUNT MEN IN SHORT SUPPLY

Topflight theatrical stunt men are becoming scarce as their generation ages and few good newcomers are appearing to fill the gap. Agencies' books have plenty of so-called stuntmen, but in the bar room brawls, the lower echelons mill about swapping pulled punches on the sawdust floor whilst the stunt elite smash each other through the banisters, down the stairs and out of the swing doors into the street beyond. Members of this elite now number little more than two dozen. They learnt their trade in the days between 1939 and 1945 with commandos and paratroopers showing them how to fight with bayonets and bare hands, to fall softly from heights and to drive vehicles safely at breakneck speed.

There is no upper age limit for stunt men, but many are approaching 40 and thinking of less taxing careers - directing the high diver when and where to fall rather than that of the diver himself. The qualities needed are courage, of course, but nerve, physical fitness and a sense of timing are essential. Stunt men must have brains, or they won't last very long.

With the return of the epic picture, stunts have become more demanding. The elite stuntman must now be prepared to joust at full tilt with a piano wire anchored to his back to jerk him from his horse at the moment of impact of his opponent's lance, handle a chariot and four, fling himself backwards into the sea off Scotland in the middle of a winter's night from 80ft up a ship's mast, or storm a castle wall in a rain of plastic boulders and be tossed off the ladder into the moat below. Careful planning and the liberal employment of mattresses and bales of straw reduce some of the risks of injury and death, but the dangers are still great.

# Nov 5th - 11th 1963

## IN THE NEWS

**Tuesday 5** — **"Guy Fawkes Clashes"** More than 120 revellers were arrested in Trafalgar Square after clashes with the police. Earlier, teenagers were turned back from trying to swim in the fountain outside the gates at Buckingham Palace.

**Wednesday 6** — **"US Convoy Moves on into Berlin"** The Russians climbed down in the 'Berlin war of nerves' and allowed an American Army convoy, held up on the Berlin Autobahn for 41 hours, to drive on without lowering the tailboards of their lorries as earlier demanded.

**Thursday 7** — **"Sheffield Chief Constable and CID Head Suspended"** The two, formerly members of a special crime squad, were found, *'undoubtedly guilty of maliciously inflicting grievous bodily harm of a serious nature on two prisoners in custody'*.

**Friday 8** — **"Labour Triumph Over Tories at Luton"** Ladbrokes bookmakers changed their odds for the General Election. Labour 7-2 on from 2-1 on, Tories 5-2 against from 6-4 against and Liberals to 250-1 against from 100-1 against.

**Saturday 9** — **"US to Quit Two More Bases Here"** America is to cut her nuclear bomber force by 19 B47 Jets when their bases at Fairford and Greenham Common are handed back to the RAF next July.

**Sunday 10** — **"Beatles in Blue Fool the Fans"** The 'fab four' avoided hundreds of screaming fans outside Birmingham Hippodrome by arriving at the stage door, dressed in policemen's helmets and dark raincoats, in a Black Maria.

**Monday 11** — **"Booming Mines"** The National Coal Board will sell more than 200 million tons of coal this year, the first time the 'magic target' has been reached and passed in three years.

## HERE IN BRITAIN

### "Saved in the Cabbage Patch"

A Trans-Canada DC 8 carrying 89 passengers and eight crew, ran off the runway while taking off at London Airport in fog. It came to rest in a field of cabbages where much of the aircraft's fuel was spilled, one engine caught fire, the whole plane was seriously damaged.

Luggage rained down from the fuselage but all the passengers were safely evacuated by escape chute with, miraculously, only three minor injuries. It was soft mud that saved a worse accident but for 45 minutes the passengers wandered around the field lost in thick fog, until the fire engines, ambulances and police found them.

## AROUND THE WORLD

### "Wunder-von-Lengede"

On 7 November, 11 West German miners were rescued from a collapsed mine after surviving for 14 days after the Lengede Iron Mine was flooded with muddy water when a sedimentation pond collapsed.

Out of 129 workers, 79 escaped during the first few hours but there seemed no hope for the remaining 50. However, on 1 November seven more men were saved after which rescue equipment was moved off-site and a memorial service for the missing men was scheduled for the 4th of November. Then in the 'Miracle of Lengede', the eleven remaining miners were rescued.

A special freight aircraft flew 25 tons of pink trading stamps from Oklahoma to Manchester airport at the beginning of the month for distribution to supermarkets and garages all over the country and started a Trading Stamp War. Whilst huge supermarkets Fine Fare and Pricerite began to give away S&H pink stamps, some of Britain's biggest stores made an attack on trading stamp gift schemes. They told the housewife *'you are not getting something for nothing, in the end you will be the loser'.*

Sainsbury's took out whole page advertisements on the matter '...Trading Stamps are bought from Trading Stamp Companies by grocers, as much as 12/- per 1,000. The grocer gives you stamps according to your purchase. You stick them into a book, collect them week after week, and when you have saved a great many, you may exchange them for a gift. Either the quality of the food the grocer sells, his profit or his service must suffer or, his prices go up. Sainsbury's make no bones about it. *It would cost £2,000,000 a year for Sainsbury's to give Trading Stamps and we never will!'*

The National Association of Master Bakers are against them saying, *'Stamp trading would inevitably mean higher prices.'* The Distillers Company, the Co-op, the Fruit and Grocers' Federation said, *'no, the spread of stamps will only mean a price increase for housewives,"* and the National Chamber of Trade, said, "*We are opposed to stamp trading and always have been; it does not matter to us who indulges in stamp trading, it is still wrong".*

The final word goes to the Drapers' Chamber of Trade, *"It is in fact rather vulgar"* the British public *dislike and distrust imported sales promotion methods of this kind. They know there is a catch in the patter of the cheap jack on the fairground."*

# Nov 12ᴛʜ - 18ᴛʜ 1963

## IN THE NEWS

**Tuesday 12**  **"Girls in the Pink"** Sperry & Hutchinson hired girls dressed all in pink to publicise their pink trading stamps at Fine Fare supermarkets whilst more trade groups including the bakers, join the fight against them.

**Wednesday 13**  **"Swift Action Against 'Rachman' Landlords"** Councils are to be given new powers to curb the profiteering of bad landlords by taking multi-occupied properties into their own c ontrol.

**Thursday 14**  **"That Was TW3 That Was"** The BBC are to end the popular satirical programme at the end of December because *'it would lose its bite in a General Election year because it is prohibited from commenting on election issues.'*

**Friday 15**  **"Fords Face a Full Stop"** A complete shutdown of Ford at Dagenham is likely, following the Electrical Trades Union call for all its 600 members at the plant to strike.

**Saturday 16**  **"Anonymous Goya Letter"** A portrait of the Duke of Wellington was stolen two years ago from the National Gallery. The letter stated, *"The Goya is still as it was when it vanished from the gallery. We are going ahead and doing the inevitable if a compromise is not met within a week."*

**Sunday 17**  **"Parson's Plea to Beatles"** A Basildon vicar has asked the Beatles to record a Christmas Carol and become the salvation of religion. "Our congregations are dwindling, yet theirs are jam packed," he said.

**Monday 18**  The new Dartford tunnel linking Purfleet in Essex with Dartford in Kent was opened for traffic. Tolls range from 6d (2p) for a bicycle, 2s 6d (12p) for a car and 6s (30p) for a lorry.

## HERE IN BRITAIN

### "Kerb Stone Measures"

A shopkeeper in Kent who was asked by a customer for a particular length of wire mesh told him, "I don't bother about a measure, but these kerb stones are about a yard." Having asked the customer to stand on the roll and run it out over the requisite number of kerb stones, the shopkeeper cut off the mesh.

However, the customer was a weights and measures inspector making a private purchase and he got more than the length he had ordered. The trader was, in spite of the error in the customer's favour, told quite firmly that kerb stones are not authorised measures.

## AROUND THE WORLD

### "The Long-Tailed Comet"

An astronomer reported in New York that a comet, Burnham 1960 II, with a 1,800,000-mile-long wagging tail is whirling in orbit round the earth. The tail moves back and forth once every four days through an arc of 15 degrees and the movement might be caused by solar wind produced when heat from the sun causes vaporisation and the comet emits radiation leaving a trail of ionised gas.

Or it could be caused by the rotation of either the head of the comet which is made of frozen methane, ammonia and some solid matter, or the nucleus which is 125,000 miles in diameter.

# A WHITE CHRISTMAS?

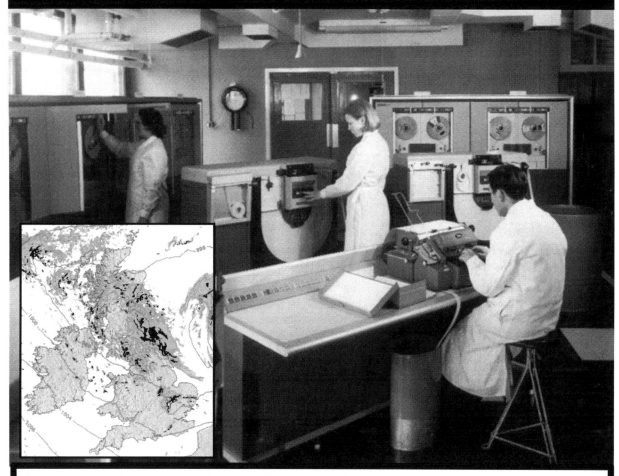

The greatest test for the men at the Met Office at the end of this month will be, 'What will the weather be like over Christmas". They are going to publish the first of their long-range weather forecasts for the month ahead. The weathermen work at the Meteorological offices in Bracknell where an existing computer called 'Meteor' will be joined by a new one, KDF9, who will enable them to calculate the barometer for 24 hours ahead. Each day a million signals flow into the headquarters from weather stations all over the world and these will now be fed into the new computer and the old-fashioned barometer will become largely redundant. But despite all their scientific skill, forecasting is still a chancy game for the weathermen, and if they are right, they very rarely get praise but if they are wrong, the wrath of the nation is made articulate.

This new service is in response to public demand but is still in its infancy. The Met Office has been making month-ahead forecasts experimentally since 1955 and over the past five years, two-thirds could be described as good; between a quarter and a fifth to have been wide of the mark but fewer than a tenth had been completely misleading. This will take the form of 30 years' averages including rainfall, temperatures and sunshine for selected places throughout Britain and there will also be a general 'prospect' for the month ahead. It will be free to press and radio and on sale to private subscribers at 1s 2d a(6p) copy.

When asked whether the experimental forecasts had indicated last winter's intense cold, the head of the Met said neither they nor anybody else foresaw that it would be the most severe for 233 years. *"I would say that that kind of forecasting, 'of catastrophe', is beyond our powers at the moment."*

# NOV 19TH - 25TH 1963

## IN THE NEWS

**Tuesday 19** **"Whirlwind Hits Village in Suffolk"** Gales and heavy rain disrupted traffic and damaged property in many parts of the country. In Orford, 12 houses were badly damaged. Electricity was restored but solid fuel fires were restricted by lack of chimney pots.

**Wednesday 20** **"Radiation Scare After Error"** The atomic energy plant at Winscale was cleared when a ' fuel stringer' was found unshielded. The advanced gas cooled reactor was closed and radiation films of all employees checked but no radiation exposures were found.

**Thursday 21** **"No Stamps With Chocolates Either"** The four largest confectionery manufacturers have all opposed stamp trading. Cadbury said, *"We feel that stamp trading in the long run is disadvantageous both to the trader and to the housewife."*

**Friday 22** **"Kennedy shot dead in Dallas"** The President of the United States has been assassinated by a gunman in Dallas, Texas. John F Kennedy was hit in the head and throat when three shots were fired at his open-topped car.

**Saturday 23** **"Johnson takes over as US president"** Fifty-five-year-old Lyndon Baines Johnson was sworn in and started his duties today. The former vice-president took his oath on the presidential plane at Andrew's Air Force Base.

**Sunday 24** **"Kennedy 'Assassin' Murdered"** Lee Harvey Oswald, the man accused of assassinating the US President, has himself been shot dead in a Dallas police station.

**Monday 25** **"John F Kennedy is Laid to Rest"** The funeral of the assassinated President took place in Washington. An estimated 800,000 Americans lined the streets to watch the coffin's procession from the Capitol.

---

### HERE IN BRITAIN

#### "Computer Built Flats"

The first block of flats to be built by British industrial methods of pre-fabrication has been opened in Kidderminster. With the supply of labour and components programmed by computer, a quarter of the normal labour was used to complete the flats in seven months at a cost of 10% less than by conventional methods.

The 12-storey block houses 44 flats that will be rented at 38s 7d a week and each flat is made of 21 prefabricated sections which are assembled on the site by a tower crane. *"Fewer than 25 men have achieved as much work as 100 men would achieve by conventional methods".*

---

### AROUND THE WORLD

#### "Nay, Nay, Thrice Nay"

A bridegroom astonished the congregation of a church at Marzano di Nola in south Italy by answering 'No' three times. The bride fainted after the priest had tried a third time and the bridegroom was heard to say clearly 'No, I have already said no'. This was followed by pandemonium in the church as he left, followed by members of his family.
Later he returned to the altar, hands clasped with the bride and gave his gave his assent. His loudly proclaimed 'Yes' was greeted with general applause. Asked later the reason for his behaviour he said that he *'must have made a mistake'.*

# ATTRACTIVE NORTHUMBRIA

The Cheviot Hills form the border with Scotland.

Seahouses is an attractive fishing port
on the North Sea Coast.

The task of turning the north-east of England into an attractive holiday area was put before delegates to a special conference where the leaders of commerce, industry and local government set about trying to find a way of breaking down the image of the area, which, they frankly admitted, was one of cold winds, grey seas, slag heaps and bad hotels. Of 32 million holidays taken by British people annually only 2.5million are spent in the north-east. The region's share has not increased for several years and 60% of the people taking holidays in the region live in it. Speakers claimed that the region could absorb an extra million visitors from outside who would bring in £10m and stimulate further industrial activity. Most of them agreed that they could never turn the land of the three rivers into a Costa Brava or make Sunderland look like San Sebastian, but there was talk of the region's 'revelationary' sunlight giving a mental and moral uplift!

Local leaders were reminded that they had considerable attractions to offer those who liked walking in the rugged country, a bracing coast offering sailing and fishing, or viewing ancient ruins and these aspects should be put across to win the region a bigger share of the £300m. The development of skiing in the Cheviots, which have good snow from mid-December to May in most winters, was one of the most attractive suggestions. When one speaker suggested 'the weather' should be forgotten in forthcoming propaganda, others claimed they had suffered from cold in Somerset, been wet through in Devon and come home to find their neighbours with rich tans acquired at Seahouses. It was further suggested that they might be able to break down that image of cold and wet by changing the name of the area from 'North-East' to 'Northumbria'.

## IN THE NEWS

**Tuesday 26**    **"Texas to Hold Inquiry into Shootings"** While the evidence against Oswald is regarded as conclusive, it is believed that Dallas police 'have adopted too cavalier an approach'.

**Wednesday 27**    **"Engineering Workers Get 5% Pay Increase"** The settlement is a victory for women workers, who in the past have usually been given the same increase as unskilled men, as they are to have the same rise as the semi-skilled.

**Thursday 28**    **"Thames Shipping Halted by Fog"** With visibility down to 25 yards, road, rail, river and air traffic suffered delays and cancellations and the European Cup Winner's match between Tottenham and Manchester United at White Hart Lane was postponed.

**Friday 29**    **"Fishing Limit Extended"** Exclusive fishing rights in British coastal waters will be extended from the present three miles to 12 miles. British trawlers have suffered from extensions in recent years by Iceland, Norway and Denmark. The Russians fixed their limit at 12 miles long ago.

**Saturday 30**    **"New British Missile Test Success"** A low-level air-launched missile has been successfully tested at Woomera, Australia. It is a development of the Blue Steel missile, now in service with RAF Bomber Command.

**Sunday Dec 1**    **"Shopping War Gets Hotter"** Washing machine magnate, John Bloom, announced he will give *cash* or goods for trading stamps from his new 'Supa Golden Stamps' company. Each book of 1,240 stamps will be worth between 10/- (50p) and 12/- (60p) in cash.

**Monday 2**    **"President's Earlier Meetings"** The Prime Minister will not meet Mr Johnson in Washington until February, a month after he meets with the German and Italian leaders.

### HERE IN BRITAIN
#### "St Paul's Homage to Mr Kennedy"

In and around St Paul's Cathedral the people of Britain crowded in their thousands to honour the memory of President Kennedy. The Archbishop of Canterbury spoke of President Kennedy as *'one who touched something universal in the human heart.*
*Thinking of him we see so vividly what we admire in a human life, and what are the great causes we care about. The man: brave to the point of heroism as his actions in wartime showed, youthful beyond the age when youthfulness always lasts, tenacious when there could be no compromise, infinitely patient when the human touch could win conciliation'.*

### AROUND THE WORLD
#### "The Mad Projectionist"

The new satellite Telstar meant that Russians could witness the events associated with the assassination of President Kennedy. It was the first time that Soviet television had picked up programmes transmitted over Telstar and the article said, *"It was as if a mad film projectionist mixed up cans of film, interlacing the bitter tragedy of the great American nation with a cheap Texas thriller, a detective story and comics.... Only the darkest Spanish Inquisition could have produced the scenes that were flashed by the American satellite"* *"We have seen the grief of the American nation and profoundly sympathise with it".*

# AN EXPENSIVE MANOEUVRE

British Army on the Rhine troops on 'realistic' autumn exercises left a trail of damage for which Germany is claiming £357,000 compensation. The sum represents nearly £40 worth of damage for each of the 9,000 soldiers, of three brigades, who took part in the six to eight weeks exercise in Schleswig Holstein in September and October. There are said to be 1,148 individual, civilian, claims. Farmers complain that their crops were flattened with one man saying his prize-winning cows were so badly frightened that the quality of their milk was affected for a month.

Car and lorry owners are claiming compensation for road accidents in which British troops were involved. There were 82 collisions between German civilian vehicles and Army trucks and tanks. House owners report that showers of plaster came down when 65-ton Centurion tanks rumbled through the streets.

However, most of the money is claimed for roads churned up by the Centurions tracks and the subsequent clearing of the muddied roads. Local people were angry about the 'carelessness of the troops' but others realise they are in Germany to defend them and they 'must have somewhere to train'. It was the first major manoeuvre carried out by BAOR in the area since 1960 and was carried out in very bad weather, almost continuous rain, which the army says was the major reason for so much damage. A Rhine Army spokesman said, *"Experience shows that these claims are considerably in excess of the actual figures!"* and under existing NATO agreements, when the claims have been individually investigated and approved, Britain will pay three-quarters of the bill and the German Federal Government the rest. Unlike the farmers, the local authorities in Schleswig- Holstein are understood to have made no protests about the conduct of the manoeuvres.

# DEC 3RD - DEC 9TH 1963

## IN THE NEWS

**Tuesday 3**    **"Rail Unions Expect Large Pay Offer"** Dr Beeching, chairman of the British Railways Board, is expected to make a substantial pay offer, the cost of which will be about £30m a year and will inevitably fall on the passenger as higher fares.

**Wednesday 4**    **"British Built A-Submarine Launched"** The Valiant, the Royal Navy's first all-British nuclear submarine, was named with 'Empire Wine' at the Vickers-Armstrong yard at Barrow in Furness.

**Thursday 5**    **"£7m Order for Concord"** Orders for two Anglo-French Concord supersonic airliners, the first order from outside the United States, has been placed by Middle East Airlines, Lebanese Air Liban. This brings the total of Concords on order by five airlines to 19.

**Friday 6**    **"Cadbury's Stop Supplies to Tesco"** In the on-going 'stamp wars', Tesco has not given an undertaking to stop giving trading stamps with Cadbury's goods. *"We shall continue to sell Cadbury's products, giving stamps with them, until supplies run out. Then we shall replace them with our own branded products".*

**Saturday 7**    **"Christine Keeler in Holloway"** At the Old Bailey she was found guilty of perjury and conspiracy in the 'Lucky Gordon' case and sentenced to 9 months in prison.

**Sunday 8**    **"Big Blaze at BEA's New Terminal"** More than 200 firemen with 30 pumps and eight turntables fought a fire at British European Airways' new £5m air terminal.

**Monday 9**    **"Freezing Fog and Ice"** 19 counties were affected last night, mostly in southern England, whilst Great Yarmouth firemen had an unusual call for December, a grass fire broke out on the marshes on the outskirts of the town.

### HERE IN BRITAIN
#### "Changes At London Zoo"

The London Zoo is to have a new house for small mammals incorporating the results of the latest scientific research. On display will be about 400 animals with 130 jumping, running, climbing, flying and aquatic species.

In the basement, day will be turned into night by a lighting system which will enable nocturnal animals to be seen at their most active by daytime visitors. Two years' study has gone into the design. The animals will be displayed to a greater degree and also live in better conditions. "An unhappy animal is a bad exhibit and makes the people who see it unhappy".

### AROUND THE WORLD
#### "Pacific Cable Commonwealth Link"

The Queen in a recorded message officially opened the Pacific section of the Commonwealth telephone cable, between Australia, New Zealand, Fiji and Canada. In her message the Queen said that a new link had been forged between the peoples of the northern and southern hemispheres and her message travelled 16,000 miles across two oceans and a continent, the greatest distance covered by a cable anywhere in the world. Plans for extending the cable include another 80-circuit system, in South-East Asia to join Australia with Hong Kong and Singapore by way of New Guinea and North Borneo.

# AXE FALLS ON ARSENAL

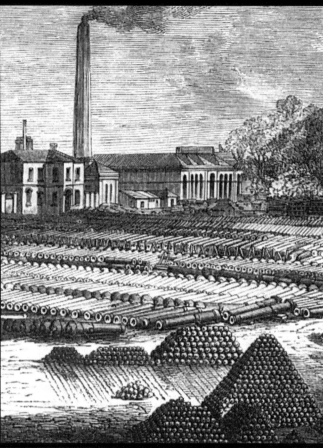

Over the next two years, the Woolwich Arsenal where armaments have been made for Britain for centuries, is to close. The long association of artillery with Woolwich began with the setting up of a gun depot there in the reign of Elizabeth 1st. Then in 1696, during the reign of William III, the 'Royal Laboratory' was established in The Warren, Tower Place, for the manufacture of ammunition and fireworks. The following year 'New Carriage Yard', where old gun carriages were repaired or scrapped, appeared and in 1716 the 'Royal Brass Foundry' was built for casting brass guns.

By the time George III paid his first visit to Woolwich in 1773, the Warren was headquarters to the 'Royal Regiment of Artillery' and the 'Royal Military Academy' as well as workshops and factories for the manufacture, proof, inspection and storage of cannon and shot. The officers came to exert considerable influence on the manufacture of guns and ammunition. George III named it the 'Royal Arsenal' in 1805 and it comprised the 'Royal Carriage Department', the 'Royal Laboratory', the proof butts and the 'Royal Brass Foundry', later the Royal Gun Factory.

The Napoleonic and Crimean Wars increased activity on the site, which expanded eastwards and by the beginning of the 20th Century, the increase in activity in the armament world, the growing complexity of weapons and in particular the serious faults in the ammunition used by the British Army in the Boer War, led to the establishment of the 'Chemical Research Department'. By then the Royal Arsenal covered 1,285 acres and stretched for three miles along the Thames, reaching its peak of production during the First World War, when it employed close to 80,000 people. During the Second World War production was distributed among other Royal Ordnance Factories nationwide, because of the risk of air attack.

## IN THE NEWS

**Tuesday 10** **"Zanziba Independence Celebrations"** The Duke of Edinburgh joined the celebrations and wished Zanzibar "a happy, peaceful, and prosperous future as an independent state within the Commonwealth."

**Wednesday 11** **"Kenya Independence Celebrations"** The Duke of Edinburgh read a message from the Queen in which she recalled her last visit to Kenya in 1952 and "On this momentous day Kenya takes her place among the sovereign nations of the world"

**Thursday 12** **"£50,000 More Train Raid Money Found"** Two sacks containing bundles of banknotes, believed to be part of the proceeds of the great train robbery last August, were found by Scotland Yard detectives in a telephone kiosk in London after an anonymous tip-off.

**Friday 13** **"New Tory Disaster"** In another by-election shock for the Government, the 7,430 majority in Dumfries was almost wiped out, slumping to 971 in one of the safest and staidest of Scottish seats.

**Saturday 14** **"Four Percent? No Thank You"** Leaders of the three railway unions rejected an offer from the British Railways Board to increase their members' pay by up to 4.8%.

**Sunday 15** **"Eight Rescued from New Volcanic Island"** They landed on the island to protest against Iceland's decision to call it "Surtsey". The Vestmann Islanders want it to be named "West Island" and were stranded when the crater erupted.

**Monday 16** **"Houses Swept Away in US Dam Burst"** The dam of a reservoir in a residential area of Los Angeles let loose a wall of water 30ft high. The floods swept away several hundred houses in the canyon below, laying waste more than a square mile of land.

### HERE IN BRITAIN

#### "Drinking More, Smoking Less"

The annual Customs and Excise report shows consumption of wine continued to go up in 1962/3 with a total of 22m gallons, an increase of well over 1m gallons on the standing record created in 1961, and the largest increase was in Spanish white wine.

More spirits were also drunk, up by more than 16m proof gallons which works out on average at four bottles for every adult. But the increase went to whisky and imported spirits, not to gin. Less tobacco was consumed, possibly because of the use of filter tips and reports that smoking is connected to lung cancer.

### AROUND THE WORLD

#### "The Sinatra Mystery"

After a tearful reunion, Frank Sinatra Junior faced television cameras and 200 reporters with his mother Nancy and sister Tina but refused to give any details of the 53 hours he spent as a kidnap victim. He said he could not talk until he had been fully interviewed by the FBI.

Young Sinatra, the 19-year-old singer, was allegedly kidnapped at gunpoint from a Lake Tahoe motel and says he was kept blindfolded and drugged for two days before being freed after his father had arranged for the ransom money of $240,000 (£85,700) to be left at a spot in Los Angeles.

# A New European Island

The new volcanic island off the south coast of Iceland is the first new European island of the century. Fishermen first saw the cloud of steam rising out of the sea on the morning of November 14. Later that day, the steam cloud had reached a height of more than 20,000ft and lava fragments were being violently ejected several thousand feet into the air. By the end of the first day of visible eruption, the lava fragments flung out from the sub-marine fissure had built a mound more than 400ft high rising from the sea floor to reach the surface and the new island had appeared.

Lava spewed out at an average rate of 500,000 tons an hour being fragmented and carried high into the air by clouds of steam caused by sea water pouring into the crater. The larger masses of red-hot lava could be seen crashing back on to the crater rim and smaller pieces were being carried thousands of feet into the air, to fall like rain on the leeward side of the volcano, sometimes as far as 20 miles or more from it. A violent contest was underway between the emerging lava building up the new island and the turbulent sea wearing it away. In 1783 a similar eruption occurred 30 miles off the south-west coast of Iceland and the resulting island was destroyed within a year. But it seems this island has become as permanent as are any of the Vestmann Islands, a little cluster of which the new one is now the most outlying member, which have already survived for some 5,000 to 10,000 years since they were formed by volcanic eruptions. They form a little group of about a dozen and their rocks rising abruptly, like an irregular row of giant teeth, are a few miles out from the coast of Iceland.

## IN THE NEWS

**Tuesday 17**    **"Mystery Mark on BEA Comet"** A score mark on the fuselage of a Comet airliner caused BEA to order their jet pilots to fly at a reduced height whilst an investigation is carried out to find the cause.

**Wednesday 18**    **"Shipyards Set the Pace"** The unions won their biggest victory so far in the 20-year-long campaign for a 40-hour week. The employers unexpectedly agreed to introduce it in two stages for their 200,000 workers.

**Thursday 19**    **"Britain's Baby Boom"** Figures show that last year's record of 840,600 live births is to be beaten, by at least 20,000. This is giving the Government planners a headache.

**Friday 20**    **"Unions Accept 6%"** The Rail Unions have said 'Yes' to Mr Beeching's Christmas offer but are counting on more to come later and will launch a new pay claim in the New Year.

**Saturday 21**    **"Stateless Man Can Stay for a Month"** Mr Denes Gyevi, the stateless refugee, has been granted a temporary stay in Britain. He was born in territory which changed hands between Hungary and Yugoslavia and inquiries are continuing into his origin.

**Sunday 22**    **"Violence Flares Again in Cyprus"** After Turkish Cypriots began gathering in their sector of Nicosia, fierce gun battles broke out, shattering a day of uneasy calm after weekend clashes between the Turkish and Greek communities.

**Monday 23**    **"Cruise Liner Ablaze"** The Greek liner Lakonia left Southampton on a cruise with 600 holiday makers onboard. She caught fire about 100 miles north of Madeira. Passengers had to abandon ship and 24 people died and 135 were missing.

### HERE IN BRITAIN

**"Swill Bins Show Room for Improvement"**

A report by London borough public health inspectors' states that the average price of luncheon vouchers is now so low that many caterers faced with rising costs find their ingenuity increasingly taxed to provide a meal within these limits. Inevitably, therefore, the City workers must be reconciled to higher prices if they wish the existing facilities to remain unimpaired.

The report adds that, judging from the amount of food which finds its way into the pig-swill bin, "it would appear that there is room for improvement in the exercise of the culinary skills in some of the thousand catering establishments situated within the city."

### AROUND THE WORLD

**"Author to Eat His Book"**

Alfred Fabre-Luce, the author, was fined 1,500 francs (£10) in a Paris court today for utterances deemed offensive to the President of the Republic in his book Haute Cour, which portrays a fictitious trial of General de Gaulle. The court ordered all copies of the book, which was banned last year, to be destroyed.

M Fabre-Luce said he would abide by the court's decision. "I have one copy left", he said, "and I propose to burn it in the Place de la Concorde on Christmas Eve. I shall pour liquor over it like a Christmas pudding and try to eat it."

# A CHRISTMAS TRUCE

For the first time since the building of the Berlin wall in August 1961, some west Berliners will be able to visit their relations in the eastern sector over Christmas and the New Year. About 400,000 west Berliners, who are separated from parents, children, grandparents, grandchildren, brothers or sisters, aunts or uncles, nieces or nephews in the east, will be allowed to cross the border between 7am and midnight. More than 24,500 west Berliners filed applications on the first day the forms were issued by east Berlin postal employees. The passes are available until January 5th and valid for one day only.

On December 19, as early as 5.30 am, west Berliners began to enter the eastern sector and whether travelling on foot or by car, they were checked through smoothly and rapidly by the east German police and frontier guards, but there was nothing like a rush of people to get across. By midday, 3,000 only had gone over although the east German authorities announced that they had already handed out more than 60,000 passes, making it possible for 160,000 to 170,000 people to visit the eastern sector (several members of one family can be allowed through on one pass).

The real rush will probably be at Christmas or at the New Year. In west Berlin some 23,000 people were again queueing in front of the 12 schools and sport halls where the applications for passes are being handled. In order to keep the crowds to a reasonable figure, many were told that they should return home, and that they would be summoned. Many, however, went on queueing. In the manufacturing district of Wedding in north Berlin, some had even stayed throughout the night, keeping themselves warm with hot drinks and spirits and dancing to music from transistor radios.

# DEC 24TH - DEC 31ST 1963

## IN THE NEWS

**Tuesday 24**      "**British Soldier Shot in Cyprus**" Renewed pleas to stop the fighting were made after a British soldier who was attempting to rescue a Greek family cut off in the Turkish sector of the east coast town of Larnaca and bring them home became the first British casualty in the Cyprus civil war.

**Wednesday 25** "**Black Christmas on the Roads**" It was the worst Christmas Day for four years with thirty-four people killed bringing the holiday road-deaths to a total of 94.

**Thursday 26**    "**A Million Dollar Snag for Liz**" Elizabeth Taylor's negotiations for a divorce hit a snag when her husband Eddie Fisher refused her offer of a million-dollar (£350,000) settlement, delaying her marriage now to Richard Burton.

**Friday 27**      "**British Troops Leave for Cyprus**" The British joined troops from Cyprus, Greece and Turkey to help restore peace in Cyprus.

**Saturday 28**    "**12 Vehicles in M1 Pile Up**" Fourteen people injured but, miraculously, no one was killed.

**Sunday 29**      "**James Meredith to Study in Nigeria**" The Negro whose admission brought about the integration of the University of Mississippi, has decided to go to Nigeria to continue his education.

**Monday 30**      "**Lakonia Sinks in 2,200 Fathoms**" The Greek cruise liner caught fire on 23 December. Total passengers and crew, 1,028; survivors, 901; known dead, 96, unaccounted for, 31.

**Tuesday 31**     "**Car Output a Record**" Car production figures released by the Board of Trade yesterday confirm the forecast that 1963 will be a record year for the British motor industry.

## HERE IN BRITAIN

### "Coming Years Full of Hope"

The Queen's Christmas Day message, recorded in advance for broadcasting, was comparatively short this year. Her voice was heard on television, but she did not appear because she is expecting her fourth child in the new year. The text included, "Since my last message of Christmas greetings to you all the world has witnessed many great events and sweeping changes, but they are already part of the long record of history. Now, as ever the important time for mankind is the future. The coming years are full of hope and promise and their course can still be shaped by our will and action."

## AROUND THE WORLD

### "Berlin Guards Shoot Boy on Wall"

Communist frontier guards shot an east German youth as he was climbing over the Berlin wall only a few hundred yards from one of the crossing-points opened to allow west Berliners to visit their relatives in the eastern sector over Christmas. He was trying to escape to the west with a colleague of the same age. As dusk gathered the two got through the preliminary barbed wire entanglements and reached the wall opposite the American sector, without being noticed but clambering on to the wall, Paul Schultz was shot in the back. His companion was unhurt and was pulled to safety.

# QUIET DUSTBINS AT NIGHT

The hunt is on for flannel-footed dustmen. St. Marylebone's public cleansing department have sent their men into a limited area of the borough to make collections between 6.30pm and 3am. This has proved an outstanding success. No longer do dustmen, rubbish, traffic, shoppers and policemen become inextricably entangled, nor do their lorries block the streets, but there is one snag. The area tested is mainly industrial and the department quails at the thought of dustmen and steel dustbins in the residential areas where the crunch of heavy feet and the crash of metal lids might prove too much. Noise meter recordings register, at midday in the middle of Piccadilly Circus, between 70 and 85 decibels, but lids being dropped on steel dustbins, 91 decibels.

The leader of the Marylebone department has invented a dustbin which he thinks will be virtually noiseless called the "plastic metal combination hinge-lidded bin", more simply known as "mechanically operated dustless enclosed loading", and 6,000 of these are to begin use within the next few weeks. Fulham has ordered 11,000 and expects to increase this to 40,000 but feels that even with plastic dustbins the noise of night collections would still be too much for residents. Apart from the lack of noise, another advantage of the new dustbins is that they are 17lb lighter than the steel bins and their shutter mechanism eliminates the spilling of dust and rubbish on pavements. Another advantage of night collections is that the average day team can collect about 38 tons of rubbish using five vehicles on three days a week, but the night team collects 50 tons using only one vehicle on five nights.

But a word of caution from the City of Westminster who have had many years of collecting rubbish at night, they say, "however much flannel is wrapped around the dustman's feet", there are always complaints about noise.

# 1963 Calendar

## January

| S | M | T | W | T | F | S |
|---|---|---|---|---|---|---|
| | | 1 | 2 | 3 | 4 | 5 |
| 6 | 7 | 8 | 9 | 10 | 11 | 12 |
| 13 | 14 | 15 | 16 | 17 | 18 | 19 |
| 20 | 21 | 22 | 23 | 24 | 25 | 26 |
| 27 | 28 | 29 | 30 | 31 | | |

## February

| S | M | T | W | T | F | S |
|---|---|---|---|---|---|---|
| | | | | | 1 | 2 |
| 3 | 4 | 5 | 6 | 7 | 8 | 9 |
| 10 | 11 | 12 | 13 | 14 | 15 | 16 |
| 17 | 18 | 19 | 20 | 21 | 22 | 23 |
| 24 | 25 | 26 | 27 | 28 | | |

## March

| S | M | T | W | T | F | S |
|---|---|---|---|---|---|---|
| | | | | | 1 | 2 |
| 3 | 4 | 5 | 6 | 7 | 8 | 9 |
| 10 | 11 | 12 | 13 | 14 | 15 | 16 |
| 17 | 18 | 19 | 20 | 21 | 22 | 23 |
| 24 | 25 | 26 | 27 | 28 | 29 | 30 |
| 31 | | | | | | |

## April

| S | M | T | W | T | F | S |
|---|---|---|---|---|---|---|
| | 1 | 2 | 3 | 4 | 5 | 6 |
| 7 | 8 | 9 | 10 | 11 | 12 | 13 |
| 14 | 15 | 16 | 17 | 18 | 19 | 20 |
| 21 | 22 | 23 | 24 | 25 | 26 | 27 |
| 28 | 29 | 30 | | | | |

## May

| S | M | T | W | T | F | S |
|---|---|---|---|---|---|---|
| | | | 1 | 2 | 3 | 4 |
| 5 | 6 | 7 | 8 | 9 | 10 | 11 |
| 12 | 13 | 14 | 15 | 16 | 17 | 18 |
| 19 | 20 | 21 | 22 | 23 | 24 | 25 |
| 26 | 27 | 28 | 29 | 30 | 31 | |

## June

| S | M | T | W | T | F | S |
|---|---|---|---|---|---|---|
| | | | | | | 1 |
| 2 | 3 | 4 | 5 | 6 | 7 | 8 |
| 9 | 10 | 11 | 12 | 13 | 14 | 15 |
| 16 | 17 | 18 | 19 | 20 | 21 | 22 |
| 23 | 24 | 25 | 26 | 27 | 28 | 29 |
| 30 | | | | | | |

## July

| S | M | T | W | T | F | S |
|---|---|---|---|---|---|---|
| | 1 | 2 | 3 | 4 | 5 | 6 |
| 7 | 8 | 9 | 10 | 11 | 12 | 13 |
| 14 | 15 | 16 | 17 | 18 | 19 | 20 |
| 21 | 22 | 23 | 24 | 25 | 26 | 27 |
| 28 | 29 | 30 | 31 | | | |

## August

| S | M | T | W | T | F | S |
|---|---|---|---|---|---|---|
| | | | | 1 | 2 | 3 |
| 4 | 5 | 6 | 7 | 8 | 9 | 10 |
| 11 | 12 | 13 | 14 | 15 | 16 | 17 |
| 18 | 19 | 20 | 21 | 22 | 23 | 24 |
| 25 | 26 | 27 | 28 | 29 | 30 | 31 |

## September

| S | M | T | W | T | F | S |
|---|---|---|---|---|---|---|
| 1 | 2 | 3 | 4 | 5 | 6 | 7 |
| 8 | 9 | 10 | 11 | 12 | 13 | 14 |
| 15 | 16 | 17 | 18 | 19 | 20 | 21 |
| 22 | 23 | 24 | 25 | 26 | 27 | 28 |
| 29 | 30 | | | | | |

## October

| S | M | T | W | T | F | S |
|---|---|---|---|---|---|---|
| | | 1 | 2 | 3 | 4 | 5 |
| 6 | 7 | 8 | 9 | 10 | 11 | 12 |
| 13 | 14 | 15 | 16 | 17 | 18 | 19 |
| 20 | 21 | 22 | 23 | 24 | 25 | 26 |
| 27 | 28 | 29 | 30 | 31 | | |

## November

| S | M | T | W | T | F | S |
|---|---|---|---|---|---|---|
| | | | | | 1 | 2 |
| 3 | 4 | 5 | 6 | 7 | 8 | 9 |
| 10 | 11 | 12 | 13 | 14 | 15 | 16 |
| 17 | 18 | 19 | 20 | 21 | 22 | 23 |
| 24 | 25 | 26 | 27 | 28 | 29 | 30 |

## December

| S | M | T | W | T | F | S |
|---|---|---|---|---|---|---|
| 1 | 2 | 3 | 4 | 5 | 6 | 7 |
| 8 | 9 | 10 | 11 | 12 | 13 | 14 |
| 15 | 16 | 17 | 18 | 19 | 20 | 21 |
| 22 | 23 | 24 | 25 | 26 | 27 | 28 |
| 29 | 30 | 31 | | | | |

Printed in Poland
by Amazon Fulfillment
Poland Sp. z o.o., Wrocław
11 April 2023

1e3a748c-bab9-4dab-bcee-588712472c71R01